THE
MARRIAGE
BUILDER

Books by Lawrence J. Crabb, Jr. . . .

Basic Principles of Biblical Counseling
Effective Biblical Counseling
Encouragement
The Adventures of Captain Al Scabbard, Nos. 1 and 2
(with Lawrence J. Crabb, Sr.)

THE MARRIAGE BUILDER

A Blueprint for Couples and Counselors

Lawrence J. Crabb, Jr.

P.O. BOX 544
WINONA LAKE, IN 46590

THE MARRIAGE BUILDER: A Blueprint for Couples and Counselors
Copyright © 1982 by The Zondervan Corporation

Zondervan Publishing House,
1415 Lake Drive, S.E.,
Grand Rapids, Michigan 49506

Library of Congress Cataloging in Publication Data

Crabb, Lawrence J.
    The marriage builder.
    Includes index.
    1. Marriage—Religious aspects—Christianity.
I. Title
BV835.C7 1982   248.8'4   82-16080
ISBN 0-310-22580-9

Edited by James E. Ruark
Designed by Louise Bauer

86 87 88 89 90 91 92 / 16 15 14 13 12

Contents

Introduction

Solomon wrote, "Is there anything of which one can say, 'Look! This is something new'? It was here already, long ago; it was here before our time" (Eccl. 1:10).

Another book on marriage. Could there possibly be anything new in this one? Isn't it time we stop writing books that dress up old truth in modern fashion and just get on with doing what we already know to do? Will Solomon's complaint be a fitting epitaph to this discussion of marriage?

More than once I have pictured the wise but weary king of Israel slowly wandering through a modern Christian bookstore, searching for real help in repairing his many marital fractures. In my imagination, after several hours of thumbing through scores of books with eye-catching dust jackets that promise to "revolutionize your marriage," old Solomon ambles toward the door with slumped shoulders and sighs, "Of making many books there is no end, and much study wearies the body" (Eccl. 12:12).

Daydreams like this compel me to explain why I have written one more book under the threat of Solomon's sigh.

In my counseling, I am often troubled to see husbands and wives locked into patterns of relating that destroy any hope of developing a deeply satisfying closeness in their marriages. Whenever I stand before a Sunday morning congregation to preach, I look out upon many well-dressed couples sharing hymnals and singing praise to the Lord for His gift of abundant and eternal life, and I suspect that very few are experiencing substantial intimacy. But a large majority of these people are professing Christians who would report that they are sincerely trying to develop their marriage according to biblical principles.

7

Why, then, are marriages so often filled with tension, bitterness, distance, shallow satisfactions, routineness, and short-lived moments of romance? Why do I sometimes face a problem within my own marriage and, after earnest prayer and brutal self-examination, remain unsure how to respond to my wife in a way that will deepen our oneness?

Are there real solutions that will develop true intimacy? Or must we resign ourselves to publicly reciting appropriate phrases about how God designed marriage while privately wondering why these sacred principles don't really work? Many of us have read dozens of books on family relationships. We've listened to the "best" evangelical speakers on the Christian home. And we have been richly blessed and helped. But somehow a cloud remains. Something still isn't quite together. Why?

I believe that part of the answer to these troubling questions lies in some dangerous underlying trends in our thinking about Christian marriage. These trends have enough truth in them to disguise their insidious errors. Much of the evangelical community appears to have unconsciously accepted certain ideas that are subtly undermining the effect of good biblical teaching on the family. As I counsel with couples puzzled over their inability to make their marriages work, I usually perceive the influence of one or more of four wrong ideas.

1. Perhaps the trend that concerns me most is the assumption that *the Bible reduces complicated issues to a few easily solved problems.* We live in the day of instant remedies. One little pill changes restless insomnia to peaceful sleep. Television shows portray dilemmas in family life that regularly get resolved before the final commercial. I wonder how many of us have come to expect quick and simple solutions to our marital problems and look for a "one-two-three" formula for straightening out badly twisted relationships.

One problem contributing to this simplistic thinking is a well-intentioned overreaction to the tendency of many professional counselors to excuse sinful living on grounds of psychological complexity. It is regrettable that many Christian psychologists talk more about such things as unconscious motivation and emotional damage than they do about sin and responsibility. The net effect is to weaken the influence of the Bible's insistence that we choose to live righteously. A number of Christians—and I am among them—react strongly to any view that explains sinful behavior as the understandable consequence of psychological forces. This concern has resulted in two polarized camps: one group, preoccupied with deep processes of human functioning, holds that sinful living is less the result of rebellious unbelief than the symptom of emotional disorder; the other group focuses its attention on conscious, intentional choices, insisting that problems of living are explained solely in terms of willful acts of sin.

In the latter view, if a husband criticizes his wife, the matter essentially comes down to whether he will choose to put off the old man with its fleshly bitterness and put on the new man characterized by love and gentleness. If he does not treat his wife in a Christlike manner, he is regarded, not as emotionally disturbed, but as stubbornly sinful. Adherents of the former view would likely probe into feelings of inadequacy, hostility toward women, and other psychological factors to determine the underlying problem behind this inappropriate behavior.

I am unalterably opposed to any line of thinking that undermines the concept of personal responsibility, and I find myself in general agreement with those who insist people are accountable for choosing godly responses to life's situations. Nevertheless, I am concerned that our renewed emphasis on responsible choices may tend to promote a superficial view of sin. Sin appears to be defined exclusively in terms of our behavior. What we *do* constitutes the sum total of our sin problem. If how we are behaving is the root problem, then it follows that the solution to difficulties like marital conflict is simple: Find out what you are doing wrong, then choose to do it right. Do something different; stop living unbiblically and start living biblically.

It is true that no Christian growth is possible without obedience. To emphasize obedience and to reject psychological thinking that understates the need for obedience is to reflect biblical truth accurately. But to concern ourselves with nothing more than *chosen acts* of obedience fails to take into account the complexity of human life as revealed in the Bible.

Naive demands that people do what they should invite token external change without real change of heart (see 2 Chron. 34:33; 7:3-4). There is more to Christian growth than forcing ourselves to respond as we should. There are other matters to attend to within the human personality in our efforts to encourage obedience.

Because our human nature is stained in every part by sin, the work of sanctification is no simple matter of "don't do it your way, do it God's way." Sin has corrupted not only what we do, but also how we think, what goals we set, and how we feel about ourselves and others. Merely changing what we do will not change who we are. The cure for the selfishness and fear that control so much of what we do cannot be reduced to shallow solutions; we need to learn how our minds deceive us. We need to understand the wrong goals we have set, honestly face how we feel, and deal with our sinful and painful emotions in a way that reflects our confidence in God's unconditional acceptance. More is needed than simplistic commands to do what we should. Programmed steps to successful family living heal the wound only slightly and fail to touch the real disease.

2. A second flaw in our views of Christian marriage (and the whole Christian life) is *the appealing emphasis on becoming happy and fulfilled.* Our peppy songs about joyful Christianity neglect the need to develop a holy, obedient walk with God no matter what personal suffering may be involved. Uppermost in the minds of many Christians, perhaps unconsciously, is a preoccupation with following Christ to achieve the abundant life of pleasant, satisfying emotions and fulfilling, enriching.opportunities.

In the last decade or so, we have dignified the shallow appeal of "be happy, feel good" by substituting the more Christian-sounding invitation to find "a fulfilling life" and to become "self-actualized." The joy and peace available to the Christian have become confused with the similar sounding but very different idea of fulfillment. This has been seized upon by our sinful natures and translated into a priority on subjectively experiencing this deep joy and a secondary concern with whether the route to fulfillment conforms to God's holy character as revealed in Scripture.

In some circles, people warmly speak of fulfillment in relationships to the point where adultery, divorce, and homosexuality are acceptable if they enhance one's own sense of meaning. "I must be happy, I must express who I am. Don't condemn me to a life of limited fulfillment. Don't box me in with your legalistic morality. Let me be Me. I must do what is best for Me. God wants me to become a whole person, and I cannot be whole within the boundaries of traditional morality."

We have become so conditioned to measuring the rightness of what we do by the quality of emotion it generates that a new version of relativistic ethics has developed that might be called the *Morality of Fulfillment.* "Fulfillment" has taken on greater urgency and value than "obedience." Psychologists do great damage by encouraging this reversal of priorities.

Does fulfillment have a place in biblical thinking? Of course.

Each of us feels a deep concern for our own well-being, and this is as it should be. I long for an ever-increasing sense of personal fulfillment, and I confess this longing with no fear that my desires are sinful. The crucial issue is not whether we should be interested in our own welfare, but rather how we believe our welfare is best served. Pursuing whatever path brings the deepest immediate sense of internal well-being appears to be a rather sensible strategy for finding fulfillment. But the Bible teaches that there is a way which—although it *seems* right to a man—in the end leads to death: the tragedy of personal emptiness and desolation. Scriptures about dying to self, finding one's life by losing it, being crucified with Christ, and living only for Christ make it clear that realizing true fulfillment depends, not on preoccupation with fulfillment, but preoccupation with knowing God through absolute surrender.

In other words, the route to fulfillment is not the one with the road sign reading "Pleasure Ahead" or "If it seems to meet your needs, keep going." The only sure path to real and lasting joy is the steep, rugged road marked "Obedience."

We have allowed a natural concern for our own satisfaction to slide into an ethic that says that whatever seems to bring happiness is right. A married woman told me recently, "I want to follow the Bible, but I just don't know if I can be happy in this relationship. He simply isn't the kind of man I can love." When we began to discuss what is involved in adhering to the Bible, it became clear that, to her, God's thoughts on what she should do were a bothersome bit of judgmental moralism. So many people close their Bibles tightly, then confidently assert that "God wants me happy and fulfilled, but I can find neither in giving myself to this marriage." How difficult it is to believe that a loving God with our deepest welfare in mind insists on painful conformity to the standards of His Word!

3. A third trend that concerns me relates closely to the second. *Psychological needs have taken over as the focus of our discussion of roles in marriage.* The Bible has been reduced to an optional guidebook as we look for ways to meet our emotional needs. As a result, the value of a plan ("Maybe I should leave my husband" or "I think I'll just not bring it up—it's better than getting into an argument") is measured not in terms of its fidelity to Scripture, but in terms of its perceived effects on people's needs and emotions. The issue of authority is really at stake here. To validate a plan of action by appealing to its potential for meeting needs is to replace the authority of an inerrant Bible with a humanistic value system.

Advice supported by statements like "This will help your marriage" or "This course of action will deepen your sense of worth as a person" carries more weight than counsel backed up by evidence that "This is what the Bible teaches." We have subtly shifted from the authority of the Bible to a new foundation for our thinking.

This humanistic foundation gives rise to two false doctrines:

a. The needs of people are of supreme importance;

b. The resources of Christianity as taught in the Bible are useful in meeting these needs.

At first glance, such a view may provoke only mild concern. After all, didn't Christ come to meet our needs? The error is subtle, but serious. In this line of thought, needy people march onto center stage, the spotlight bathes them in absorbing attention, and the God of the Bible remains in the wings calling out directions as they search for fulfillment. In biblical Christianity, it is the Person of Jesus Christ who fills the spotlight, and He graciously beckons the audience to find eternal fulfillment by becoming lost in His glory. Paul well understood Christ's terms for humanity's fulfillment when he said, "For to me, to live is Christ" (Phil. 1:21).

4. My last concern has to do with our *fragmented approach to understanding the family*. Good books on how to be a Christian husband and father abound. There are helpful books dealing tastefully and practically with a biblical view of sex. Women have been instructed in everything from motherhood to submission to finding liberation-evangelical-style to cooking for Christ. But relatively little effort has been directed recently toward developing a comprehensive understanding of God's design for marriage. Without a clear idea of the larger picture, it is easy to misconceive and distort specific responsibilities within marriage. For example, submission is often defined narrowly as "do whatever your husband says" with no thought about how submission fits into God's great plan for intimate relationships. Similarly, men sometimes regard headship as a prerogative to make demands, and they miss the point of loving leadership as God's route to building a wife's sense of security.

Many couples with whom I've counseled would benefit from grasping a biblical perspective that is broad enough to provide a clear, general idea of what marriage is really all about and practical enough to offer specific guidelines for implementing God's design for intimacy.

Now let me restate these four upsetting trends that I find are infecting much of today's thinking about the family:

1. Family problems are often regarded as simple, one-issue difficulties that can be readily resolved without teeth-gritting effort by carefully applying step-by-step formulas;

2. The appeal of many book titles is their promise of fulfillment, subtly eroding a willingness to endure hardship (especially the hardship of rejection from family members) for the sake of obedience to Christ;

3. Gluing a marriage together in a way that satisfies the participants and meets their relational needs has quietly assumed greater priority than simply doing whatever God says in the belief that obedience to His Word will meet personal needs;

4. The available literature tends toward a piecemeal strategy for fitting together the marital jigsaw puzzle; the larger picture of God's design is obscured by attending to various smaller parts of the puzzle.

To my mind, at least some of our confusion as we face family responsibilities stems from the influence of these four trends. This book represents an effort to consider marriage within a framework that specifically opposes these. Four positions are reflected throughout my discussion of the marriage relationship:

1. Reading this book will not guarantee a dramatically and rapidly changed life. Christian growth is a long, often difficult process. I offer no simple solutions or proven formulas for the many problems created by living intimately with another sinner. However, commitment to the lordship of Christ and the authority of Scripture will provide the needed motivation and strength to live responsibly. Responsible Christian living will gradually yield personal dividends of deep joy and unshakable hope.

2. Sincerely trying to live by the Bible is sometimes hard, confusing, or disillusioning. Obedience to God will likely expose you to pain that could be avoided or at least numbed if your priority were "to feel good." When I face the choice of painful obedience or comfortable compromise, Peter's words often come to mind: "Lord, to whom [else] shall we go? You have the words of eternal life" (John 6:68). The alternatives are following God or following our own preferences.

3. Commitment to living a godly life in no way guarantees that your marriage will work. Your spouse may simply refuse to cooperate. It may even be that your husband or wife would respond more warmly to you if you were willing to compromise certain Christian principles. The question to be asked when facing marital difficulties is *not* "What will make the marriage better?" but rather

"What does the Bible tell me to do?" God's Word must take priority over what I think would best meet my needs.

4. In developing a comprehensive view of marriage, the Bible must be seen as the final authority in determining the principles on which to act. The kind of cultural interpretations that limit, for example, the applicability of Paul's statements on marriage to our modern situation must be rejected. To accept such "culturalizing" of Scripture effectively substitutes the wisdom of biased human thinking for the wisdom of God. This book assumes both the inerrancy and the transcultural authority of the Bible.

As I write, my mind is filled with the faces of people who have talked with me of their marital distress. My prayer is that this book will speak clearly and helpfully to husbands and wives who desire to build an intimate marriage on a biblical foundation.

Part I
THE GOAL OF MARRIAGE

1
ONENESS:
What It Is and
Why It Is Important

Several months ago I was working on a rough draft of this book during a flight to New York City. A flight attendant noticed the words "The Goal of Marriage" written at the top of a yellow pad of paper resting on the tray table in front of me. She asked what I was writing. When I told her I was starting a book on marriage, she said, "Well, I'm glad, because I really believe in marriage. After six years of living with a man, I decided that I wanted to be married. Since the fellow I was living with liked our no-strings-attached arrangement, I found somebody else who was willing to tie the knot, and we got married two months ago. So far it's great!"

I asked her why she preferred a marriage commitment to merely living together. She thought for a few seconds, then said, "I think it's the commitment part I wanted. I married a man who seems to be really committed to loving me and working on a relationship. I never felt secure enough to really open up and try to get close with a man who wouldn't make any promises."

This incident prompts two questions: (1) What was this woman's purpose in exchanging her live-in boyfriend for a husband? (2) How was she hoping to reach her objective?

Consider a second example.

A husband in his early thirties complained to me that his wife was a disappointment to him. She was pretty and personable, a good cook, and a devoted mother to their two small children. But these qualities were offset by her constant criticizing, her impatient corrections and rebukes, and her negative attitude. Nothing he did seemed to satisfy her and, he added with a touch of noble frustration, he was the sort of husband many women would be delighted to have.

This man's wife had been staring dejectedly at the floor the whole time he was speaking. When he stopped talking, she spoke without raising her head. "What he says is true. I'm an awful nag, and I do complain a lot. I just feel so unloved by Jimmy."

When she raised her head, there was anger in her eyes.

"Sometimes he explodes at me, calling me awful names. He'll never pray with me. Sure, he smiles at me a lot, and he thinks that makes him a great husband, but I know he doesn't really accept me. His smiles always turn into pushy demands for sex; and when I won't give in to him, he throws a fit."

Reflect on this couple and ask the same two questions: (1) What was each partner longing for from the other? (2) What were their strategies for gaining their desires?

Think about one more illustration.

A middle-aged couple—Christians, attractive, talented, financially comfortable, faithful, active church members— admitted that their marriage was in trouble.

"I feel like such a hypocrite," the wife stated. "If you asked the people in our church to list the ten most happily married couples they know, our names would probably appear on every list. We're sociable, we entertain church people frequently in our beautiful home, we sing in the choir together. We really play the role—but our relationship is miserable.

"We get along—but from a distance. I can never tell him how I really feel about anything. He always gets mad and jumps at me, or he clams up for a couple days. I don't think we've ever had a really close relationship."

Her husband responded, "I don't think it's all that bad. We've got a lot going for us: the kids are doing fine, my wife teaches Sunday school, the Lord is blessing my business. That's better than a lot of—"

I interrupted. "How much do you really share yourself—your feelings, hopes, and dreams—with your wife?"

"Well," he answered, "whenever I try she usually doesn't seem all that interested, so I just don't bother."

"I'd listen if you'd really share with me!" his wife blurted. "But your idea of sharing is to lecture me on how things should be. Whenever I try to tell you how I feel, you always say something like 'I don't know why you feel like that.' I think our communication is awful."

Once more, consider the same two questions: (1) What do these emotionally divorced partners want from their marriage but have so far been unable to develop? (2) How are they trying to achieve what they both so deeply desire?

THE NEED FOR INTIMACY

Let's deal with the first question: *What was each of these people seeking?*

It is apparent that the flight attendant married in the hope that a relationship of mutual commitment would provide the intimacy she lacked with her live-in boyfriend.

The frustrated husband wanted to feel a sense of oneness with his wife but believed her critical and rejecting spirit was getting in the way. He felt angry with her, much as I would feel toward someone who, after I had gone without food for several days, blocked my path to a table spread with good things to eat. His wife felt unable to give herself warmly to a man who seemed to use rather than accept her. She desperately wanted to be close to her husband, but felt a sense of dread at the prospect of moving toward a man who perhaps didn't really love her.

The couple whose marriage was a well-decorated but empty package felt completely blocked from touching one another emotionally. The absence of real intimacy left a void for them—which she freely and bitterly acknowledged, but which he ignored by focusing on the external trappings of family success.

The newlywed stewardess, the explosive husband and his critical wife, and the couple who could not communicate were all pursuing the same elusive goal: *A deep experience of personal intimacy through relationship with a person of the opposite sex.*

Nothing reaches so deeply into the human personality as relationship. The fabric of biblical truth is woven from Genesis to Revelation with the thread of relationship:

- *Perfect relationships* within the Trinity;
- *Broken relationships* between God and man, Adam and Eve, and Cain and Abel;
- *Loving relationships* between Aquila and Priscilla, Ruth and Naomi, and Jesus and John;
- *Oppositional relationships* between Jezebel and Elijah, and Jesus and the Pharisees;
- *Strained relationships* between Abraham and Lot, and Paul and John Mark.

The kinds of emotions that develop within relationships are also vividly portrayed in Scripture:

• *Agony over lost relationships*—David weeping for Absalom; Jesus crying out, "My God, why have you forsaken me?";

• *Bitter remorse from grieving a loved one*—Peter after the cock crowed the third time;

• *The joy of reunion*—Jacob meeting Joseph in Egypt; Jairus's daughter restored to her father;

• *The relaxed enjoyment of a comfortable relationship*—Christ at the home of Mary and Martha.

The list is endless. Clearly, the biblical story presents the drama of relationship in all its fullness.

Why is the theme of relationship so prominent in the Word of God? Because only within the context of relationship can the deepest needs of human personality be met.

People everywhere long for intimate relationships. We all need to be close to someone. Make no apology for your strong desire to be intimate with someone; it is neither sinful nor selfish. Don't ignore the need by preoccupying yourself with peripheral satisfactions such as social achievement or acquiring knowledge. Neglecting your longing for relationship by claiming to be above it is as foolish as pretending you can live without food. Our need for relationship is real, and it is there by God's design.

God created us in His image, personal beings unlike all other creatures, and like Him in our unique capacity for relationship. As dependent personal beings, we cannot function fully as we are designed without close relationships. I understand the Scriptures to teach that relationship offers two elements which are absolutely essential if we are to live as God intended: (1) The *security* of being truly loved and accepted, and (2) The *significance* of making a substantial, lasting, positive impact on another person.[1]

These needs are real and must be satisfied before thoroughly biblical action is possible. It makes no sense to exhort people whose needs for security and significance are not met to live responsibly before God any more than it does to instruct someone with laryngitis to speak up. If a woman knows nothing of inward security and sees no hope of finding it, she cannot give herself to her husband in the way the Bible commands. To submit willingly to a man who is selfish and inconsiderate in his decisions, to become vulnerable to a husband who through weakness or indifference will not provide love, requires some already existing security.

Consistently loving a woman who communicates disrespect for

---

[1]See chapter 2 for a fuller discussion of these two needs.

his thinking and keeps a critical, angry, rejecting distance is impossible for a man who lacks a convinced sense of his own significance and worth. We were not intended to function according to the Master's plan without first equipping ourselves with the Master's provisions.

THE PROBLEM OF FEELINGS

To avoid misunderstanding, let me state that we do not need to *feel* secure or significant in order to function as we should. I may not *feel* worthy or accepted, but I am still responsible to *believe* what God has said. His Word assures me that in Christ I am both secure in His love and significant in His plan. A wife who *feels* desperately insecure is quite capable of giving herself to her husband if she *believes* she is secure in Christ. A husband who *feels* threatened by his wife's rejection is responsible for lovingly accepting her because he can *believe* that he is a worthwhile Christian regardless of his wife's response.

Christ has made me secure and significant. Whether I feel it or not, it is true. I am instructed by God to believe that my needs are already met, and therefore I am to live selflessly, concerned only with the needs of others. The more I choose to live according to the truth of what Christ has done for me, the more I will come to sense the reality of my security and significance in Him.

Sin has made an utter wreck of things. God's original design was that man and woman should live in fellowship with Him and in a selfless relationship of mutual giving to each other. In such a relationship my love would so thrill my wife that I would feel deeply *significant* as I realized the joy that my love creates in her; I would exult in the *security* that her love provides me. She too would find her *significance* in touching my deepest needs and would enjoy the *security* of my love for her.

But something has gone wrong in our marriage. I no longer believe that my needs are already met. I seem to think that I need my spouse to give me security and significance *before* I can respond as I should. I now *wait* for her to fill me first, *then* I give of myself to her. If she fails to come through in a way that satisfies me, I back away or perhaps attack her. To the degree that I trust her to accept me fully, I will be open and loving with her. But now my love for her depends on her love for me. And she approaches our relationship in exactly the same way. *If* I love her in a way that brings her security, *then* she gives herself in loving subjection to me. Otherwise she establishes enough distance to numb the pain of rejection.

A terrible situation results. Because I have asked my spouse to meet my needs, she now has the power to withhold what I need—and thereby to destroy me. *Fear* has entered our relationship. We have become afraid of each other. We play cat-and-mouse, wait-and-see games. Neither of us can find what we desperately need in our relationship because of fear.

Yet God intends that I become one with my wife in a relationship that deeply touches her need for security. And she is to become one with me in a way that satisfies my longing for significance and worth. God planned for our marriage to develop into an intimate relationship in which we experience the truth that our deepest personal needs for significance and security are genuinely met in Christ. When God presented Eve to her husband, the Bible tells us, they became one flesh, that is, they fully experienced a relationship of *Oneness*. Developing this kind of relationship is the goal of marriage.

The goal of oneness can be almost frightening when we realize that God does not intend that my wife and I find our personal needs met in our marriage. He also wants our relationship to validate the claims of Christianity to a watching world as an example of the power of Christ's redeeming love to overcome the divisive effects of sin. In John 17:21, Jesus poured out His heart to the Father: "I pray . . . that all of them may be one, Father, just as you are in me and I am in you. May they also be in us so that the world may believe that you have sent me." Our relationships with all fellow believers were in mind in Christ's prayer for oneness; but marriage, with its unique opportunity for intimacy, offers a convincing demonstration of the power of Christ's love to enable people to experience true relationship.

The first of our two questions can now be answered more completely. What were the stewardess and the two unhappy couples seeking? A relationship in which their deepest needs for security and significance could be substantially met.

Now, the second question: How were they trying to develop such a relationship?

Whatever strategies the two couples had followed were woefully ineffective. Neither am I confident that the flight attendant had a more successful game plan for achieving the oneness she desired.

What is an effective strategy for building a good relationship? Should you start by telling your partner everything you feel? Do you make a list of "ways to be nice this week" and do your best to follow it? Will getting up earlier to spend more time with God in devotions be helpful? Perhaps counseling or attending another seminar will do the trick. Or is the solution simply to repent of your selfishness and promise God to really do your part?

There are no simple answers. But there are answers—difficult to accept because they cut across the grain of our fallen human nature, and authoritative because they come from God's Word. The rest of this book attempts to provide these answers.

Chapters 2-4 explain the idea of oneness in order to give us a clear goal toward which to move. In part II, "Building the Foundation" (chapters 5-7), I discuss the prerequisites for reaching the goal. A later volume (part III, "Reaching Toward the Goal") will be concerned with the specific responsibilities of each partner in building an intimate relationship of oneness in which a couple's deepest needs can be met.

2
SPIRIT ONENESS:
Who Meets My Needs?

A man in his middle forties complained to me that his wife was cold, angry, and argumentative. I interrupted his recitation of her faults to say, "It sounds as if you think that because your wife is failing you so badly, you are therefore justified in your bitter attitude toward her. The Bible, however, instructs you to love your wife though she may be thoroughly disagreeable, to love her the way Christ loves His people."

He was incredulous.

"Wait a minute! Maybe I am supposed to love her—I'm sure I should. But I need a little love and respect too. She's giving me nothing but criticism and a cold shoulder, and you tell me to love her. Who's going to meet *my* needs?"

His question must not be lightly dismissed with exhortations to stop such self-centered fussing and to trust the Lord with whatever emotional bruises result from his wife's neglect. Truth reduced to the level of cliché ("Trust the Lord," "Pray about it," etc.) rarely promotes conviction or healing. This man has substantive needs that cry for satisfaction and will not quiet down under glib scolding and reminding that "Jesus is all you need."

This man was distraught and irritated as a result of his wife's failure to love him. The marriage relationship was not meeting his emotional needs. The solution to his problem seemed obvious to him: to change his wife so that she would meet his needs.

Picture the dilemma of the marriage counselor. Suppose he were to tell this man's wife that she should become more loving to her husband. Can you predict her response? "But I have needs too, and I don't feel very loved in this relationship either. Who's going to meet *my* needs for love and affection?"

To understand God's design for marriage, we must begin with the fact that both husbands and wives have legitimate personal needs which press for satisfaction.

These *personal* needs are as real as our *physical* needs. It is impossible to function effectively if these needs are not met. In this chapter I show that no marriage can ever follow the biblical pattern unless both partners have experienced satisfaction at the deepest level of their personal needs. These needs can only be met in the context of a relationship with someone else; no person can satisfy his own needs.

THE DILEMMA OF NEEDS

This state of affairs creates a dilemma. Both my wife and I have real personal needs for love and respect that must be met if we are to treat each other as we should. It follows that I cannot fully love her until I sense that I am a loved, worthwhile person. It also follows that she cannot truly love me until she knows that she is a deeply secure woman. What are we to do?

Can I rightly rebuke my wife and exhort her to do better? But I really cannot expect her to treat me properly until she feels loved. Yet I am unable to provide her with the love *she* needs until someone meets *my* needs. This situation between husband and wife is rather like two bankrupt businessmen depending on each other for the capital to begin a new partnership.

Perhaps we are both supposed to rely exclusively on the Lord to respond adequately to our longings. This answer seems sound, but it has its own set of problems. The spiritual maturity required to experience Christ's love as continually sustaining amid real emotional pain is a distant goal for many Christians. The Lord sometimes seems far off and removed from the reality of our pressing, human needs. A thirty-five-year-old woman whose husband has coldly neglected her for years has, understandably, a difficult time turning down a man who offers her a warm, close relationship that includes sexual relations. To console her with words about God's unfailing love seems rather like encouraging a starving woman by showing her magazine pictures of a well-spread dinner table; to exhort her to remain obedient to God's Word may somehow seem to deny or understate her legitimate hunger.

But suppose we commit ourselves to trusting fully in the sufficiency of Christ to meet our needs. What role, then, should our spouses assume? Is my wife to be only a concerned bystander watching from a distance as I struggle to deepen my walk with the Lord? Will her efforts to become close to God be so personal and private that I will be excluded from the realm of her innermost emotional nature? Exactly how are we to become deeply one?

Before we deal with these questions, we need to consider in greater detail the nature of personal needs.

PERSONAL NEEDS

People are more than physical bodies. The Bible clearly teaches that our skin and bones and hair and organs constitute a home in which our personal selves temporarily live. When our hearts stop beating and our bodies decompose, that identifiable entity I know as "Me" continues in a conscious and personal existence. Who is this "Me"?

Genesis 1:27 states that mankind was created in God's image. In some sense, people are like God. But God is a non-corporeal being, that is, He does not have a physical body (except, of course, through the incarnation of the Second Person of the Godhead). His essential being is not matter. Therefore our similarity to God cannot be found in our flesh and bones. My *physical* being is not like God.

But I am a *personal* being, and that is like God. God is a loving, purposeful *Person* who thinks, chooses, and feels. I too am a *person* capable of love and purpose who thinks, chooses, and feels. The Bible uses various words to describe the personal character of man, such as *soul, mind, heart* and *will*. The biblical term *spirit*, however, seems to refer to the deepest part of man's essential nature as a person. When I think about the deepest part of me—the part that has the capacity for fellowship with God—I am reflecting on my spirit. Let us consider the characteristics of this person or spirit who resides in the body.

I recently asked a group of people to close their eyes and meditate on these questions: What do I really want? What are my deepest longings? What do I most desire that would bring me the greatest joy? As they meditated, I asked them to choose one word that best expressed their longings. Among the words they offered were *acceptance, meaning, love, purpose, value,* and *worth.*

Most of us, when we look within, can put our fingers on a strong desire to love and be loved, to accept and be accepted. When we sense that someone genuinely cares about us, or when we ourselves sense a deep compassion for someone else, something profound is stirred within us. I suggest that our longing for love represents one set of needs that partly defines what it means to be a person or spirit.

If you continue to reflect on your inner desires, you may notice something else. Do you experience an intangible sense of wholeness, a feeling of vitality and fullness, when you do something important to you? Washing dishes or mowing the lawn may bore us, but wrestling with decisions of major consequence or responding to a medical emergency extends into deeper parts of our personality. We sense an urgent meaningfulness to what we are doing— nerve-shattering perhaps, but meaningful. Thus, to be a person involves a second set of needs—needs for meaning and value.

As I study personalities in the Bible, I am repeatedly impressed with the reality of these two set of needs. In Romans 8, Paul's excitement over Christ's unquenchable love seems to want to burst beyond the constraints of language. In another example, Job's confidence in a living Redeemer who will one day present Himself before his eyes nearly overwhelms him (Job 19:25-27). The apostle John is consumed by the thought of the Lord's love for His children (see especially 1 John 3:1). Ruth was bound to Naomi by a force stronger than cultural ties. Something inside these people was deeply moved by *love.* As personal, spiritual beings, made in the image of the God who is love, they all had a capacity for love that—before the fall of man into sin—was continuously and perfectly filled through unbroken fellowship with God. As soon as man was separated from God by sin, his *capacity* for love was no longer filled and was therefore experienced as a *need*—a need for love or, in the term I prefer, a need for *security.*

Abraham was willing to leave his home to travel great distances because he was looking for a city with foundations, designed and built by God (Heb. 11:8-10). There was a *point* to what he was doing that motivated him. Jeremiah endured endless persecutions and remained faithful even in despair because the *purpose* of his ministry—to honor what he knew was true—burned deeply within him (Jer. 20:9). Paul was content to postpone his entrance into heaven because he realized the value of his continued ministry on earth (Phil. 1:21-24). Each of these saints was motivated by the belief that what he was doing had meaning. As personal beings, they had a capacity for sensing purpose and value to their lives. Before he sinned, Adam's willing participation in God's purpose for him completely satisfied his capacity for experiencing a meaningful life. But after his rebellion against God's plan, his capacity for realizing the importance of his activity was felt as a need—a need for *significance*.

The intangible identity that I know as "Me" has two real and profound needs, which are substantive personal realities not reducible to biological or chemical analysis. They have a personal existence, independent of the physical body, that constitutes the core of what it means to be a spirit.

The image of God is reflected in these two needs. God is a personal being who in His essential nature is *love* and who, as a God of design and purpose, is the author of *meaning*. We too are personal beings, but unlike our infinite, self-sufficient, and perfect God, we are limited, dependent, and fallen. God *is* love; we *need* love. Whatever God does *is* significant; we *need to do* something significant.

We can state these needs succinctly:

Security: A convinced awareness of being unconditionally and totally loved without needing to change in order to win love, loved by a love that is freely given, that cannot be earned and therefore cannot be lost.

Significance: A realization that I am engaged in a responsibility or job that is truly important, whose results will not evaporate with time but will last through eternity, that fundamentally involves having a meaningful impact on another person, a job for which I am completely adequate.

Thus, being a person (or spirit) centrally involves an identity that requires security and significance to function effectively. When both these needs are met, we experience ourselves as *worthwhile* people.

My wife too is a spirit being, that is, she also needs to find security and significance. If we as a married couple are to become one at the level of our spirits—achieve what I call Spirit Oneness —then we must find some way to meet at the level of our deepest needs.

But how? And here we are back to the question posed at the

beginning of this chapter: How can husband and wife become deeply one at the level of their personal needs? It would appear that as we seek to meet our personal needs in marriage, essentially four courses of action are open to us. We may—

1. Ignore our needs;
2. Find satisfaction in achievement;
3. Attempt to meet our needs in each other;
4. Depend on the Lord to meet our needs.

Option 1: Ignore our needs.

The first option can be quickly rejected. If, as I believe the Scriptures teach, these personal needs are as real as our physical needs for food, water, and shelter, then to ignore them is to invite catastrophe. When physical needs remain unmet, we move toward *physical death.* When personal needs for security and significance are neglected and go unsatisfied, we move toward *personal death.* The symptoms of approaching personal death include feelings of worthlessness, despair, morbid fears, loss of motivation and energy, a turning to drugs or sex or alcohol to numb the pain of dying, and a sense of emptiness and boredom. We have been created with real personal needs and, to be faithful stewards of our lives, we must not ignore them.

Option 2: Find satisfaction in achievement.

Operating through a fallen world, Satan has taught us to believe a lie. Our culture encourages us to measure a person's value by his or her achievement. The world has squeezed many Christians into the mold of believing that our need for a sense of worth can be met without entering into a deep relationship with the living God.

In our society, a man's value is typically measured in terms of earning power; prestige of occupation; the location, cost, and size of his home; social personality and physical attractiveness; cars; clothing; education; and athletic talent or musical ability. In a religious context, his ministry abilities in the church (singing, teaching Sunday school, etc.) are additional standards of measurement.

For women, worth is often evaluated according to social circles; the husband's job or position; charm, poise, and graciousness; the style, brand name, and cost of clothing; home and furnishings; and public abilities (entertaining, speaking to women's groups, etc.).

Too many couples have unwittingly bought Satan's lie. The "beautiful people" who have been blessed with money, good looks, and talent may experience a counterfeit sense of worth that provides some satisfaction of their needs. Because the pain of their unmet needs is dulled, they may never enter into the difficult struggle of finding real security and significance. Their lives may appear happy, vital, and trouble-free—no morbid wrestling matches with deep inner conflict. Whenever discomfort reaches the threshold of awareness, these people anesthetize it with more activities, purchases, trips, or whatever else they enjoy.

I wonder how many Christian couples with comfortable means and interesting lives never come together at the deepest level of their personalities, but bury their inward longings for love and purpose under a mountain of success instead. How sad! How empty! Better to struggle with substance than to comfortably accept a shadow.

Following Option 2—attempting to find satisfaction in achievement rather than in the struggles of relationship—will reliably result in a shallow relationship that may feel very pleasant but will fail to unite husband and wife at their deepest level.

Option 3: Attempt to meet our needs in each other.

If ignoring our needs is dangerous and if finding counterfeit satisfaction in achievement results in shallow relationships, then what should we do with our needs? A large majority of people turn to their marriage partners for the answer.

Consider what may really be happening when a couple get married: Two people, each with personal needs pressing for fulfillment, pledge themselves to become one. As they recite their vows to love and respect each other, strong but hidden motivations stir inside them. If a tape recorder could somehow tune into the couple's unconscious intentions, I wonder if perhaps we would hear words like these:

> *Bridegroom:* I need to feel important and I expect you to meet that need by submitting to my every decision, whether good or bad; by respecting me no matter how I behave; and by supporting me in whatever I choose to do. I want you to treat me as the most important man in the world. My goal in marrying you is to find my significance through you. An arrangement in which you are commanded by God to submit to me sounds very attractive.
>
> *Bride:* I have never felt as deeply loved as my nature requires. I am expecting you to meet that need through gentle affection even when I'm growling, thoughtful consideration whether I am always sensitive to you or not, and an accepting, romantic sensitivity to my emotional ups and downs. Don't let me down.

A marriage bound together by commitments to exploit the other for filling one's own needs (and I fear that most marriages are built on such a basis) can legitimately be described as a "tic on a dog" relationship. Just as a hungry tic clamps on to a nourishing host in anticipation of a meal, so each partner unites with the other in the expectation of finding what his or her personal nature demands. The rather frustrating dilemma, of course, is that in such a marriage there are two tics and no dog!

Inevitably, as the years pass, husband and wife will occasionally touch at deep levels. One woman told me how desperate she felt when the doctor emerged from the operating room to inform her that her four-year-old daughter had just died. In that moment she knew a terrible pain that penetrated to the core of her being. When she fell into her husband's arms, he coldly pushed her away and left the hospital. She was alone at a time when she needed to know that life still had purpose. When she needed to feel the love of someone close, her husband failed her. There is no greater torment than to expose your needs so fully and receive no help. And *every* husband and wife, no matter how godly, has many times failed to provide what the other has needed.

Reflect on your marriage for a moment. Is there a feeling of hurt that you are reluctant to share directly with your spouse or perhaps a subject (like sex or time together or annoying habits) that you carefully avoid? Why? Why do we sometimes have difficulty telling our spouses how we feel or what concerns us?

Every person alive has experienced sometime the profound hurt of finding rejection when he or she longed for acceptance. We come into marriage hoping for something different, but inevitably we soon encounter some form of criticism or rejection. The pain that results is so intense that it *demands* relief. So we retreat behind protective walls of emotional distance, angry with our partners for letting us down so badly, unwilling to meet again at the level of deep needs for fear of experiencing more pain.

Perhaps this situation can be diagramed as on the following page. Protective layers are designed to prevent the rejection from getting "inside" to where we feel the hurt.

A variety of behaviors can function as protective layers. Some of the more common ones, which we will discuss in chapter 3, are—

- Unwillingness to share deep feelings;
- Responding with anger when real feelings are hurt;
- Changing the subject when the conversation begins to be threatening;

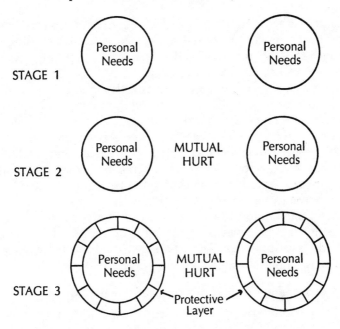

- Turning off, clamming up, or other maneuvers designed to avoid rejection or criticism;
- Keeping oneself so busy with work, social engagements, entertainment, church activities, or endless chatter that no deep sharing is possible.

Again, the point of each of these layers is to protect oneself from vulnerability to hurt at the hands of a spouse.

I am persuaded that most couples today live behind thick protective walls of emotional distance that block any hope for developing substantial oneness at the level of our deepest personal needs. What is to be done? Shouldn't we learn to be more loving and sensitive to each other? Can't we break down the barriers that separate us by accepting each other as God for Christ's sake has accepted us? Of course we should. The Bible tells us to and there-fore we can. But we can never do it perfectly.

The most accepting wife in the world cannot meet her husband's need for significance. Because she is a sinner, my wife will not always minister to me as she should; even if she were to do so, she does not have the power to make me adequate for an eternally important task—and that alone will satisfy me.

The most loving husband in the world can never meet his wife's need for security. The stain of self-centeredness has discolored every motivation within us. We are utterly incapable of providing our wives with the unconditional and selfless acceptance they require. We simply are not enough for each other.

Let me briefly restate the problems with Option 3. If I look to my wife to meet my needs, then our relationship is corrupted by (1) *manipulative efforts* to acquire what I think I need; (2) *fear* that my manipulations may not be effective; (3) *anger and pain* when they do not succeed; and (4) a nagging (perhaps unconscious) sense of *guilt* because my approach to marriage is fundamentally selfish. We will inevitably retreat from each other behind protective layers that block the development of oneness.

I am therefore forced to conclude that if my wife and I are to become one at the level of our spirit (the deepest level of our being), then we must *not* depend on each other to meet our personal needs. What are we to do?

Option 4: Depend on the Lord to meet our needs.

Our personal needs for security and significance can be genuinely and fully met only in relationship with the Lord Jesus Christ. To put it another way, all that we need to function effectively as persons (*not necessarily to feel happy or fulfilled*) is at any given moment fully supplied in relationship with Christ and in whatever He chooses to provide.

1. We need to be secure. He loves us with a love we never deserved, a love that sees everything ugly within us yet accepts us, a love that we can do nothing to increase or decrease, a love that was forever proven at the Cross, where Christ through His shed blood fully paid for our sins to provide us with the gift of an eternally loving relationship with God. In that love, I am secure.

2. We need to be significant. The Holy Spirit has graciously and sovereignly equipped every believer to participate in God's great purpose of bringing all things together in Christ. The body of Christ builds itself up through the exercise of each member's gifts. We are enabled to express our value by ministering to others, encouraging our spouses, training our children, enduring wrong without grumbling, and faithfully doing everything to the limits of our capacity for the glory of God. We can live in the confidence that God has set out a path of good works for us to follow (Eph. 2:10) and that our obedience will contribute to fulfilling the eternal plan of God. These truths, when realized and acted upon, provide unparalleled significance.

THE PLATFORM OF TRUTH

Our fourth option, then, is to depend on the Lord to meet our personal needs. We really have no other rational choice. But there are problems. Our dulled eyes of faith strain to keep these spiritual realities in clear focus. We have a remarkable capacity for failing to lay hold of ideas that I suppose would seem so clear to undiluted faith.

Spiritual truth can be compared to a balance beam, a narrow platform from which we can easily fall off either side. The central truth that serves as the platform for Christian marriage—and for all Christian relationships—is that in Christ we are at every moment eternally loved and genuinely significant.

In Christ, I am significant and secure; therefore I can live responsibly before God no matter what happens.

PLATFORM OF TRUTH

Too often Christians fall off this platform of truth into error. When key relationships (marriage, family, friendship) or life events (job, health, prestige) fail to make me *feel* secure or significant, it may be difficult to hold firmly onto the fact that I remain a worthwhile person. When a wife communicates disrespect for her husband or when a husband emotionally withdraws from his wife, it is not easy for the rejected partner to grasp with warm conviction the truth of acceptance and worth in Christ.

In Christ, I am significant and secure; therefore I can live responsibly before God no matter what happens.

PLATFORM OF TRUTH

Error 1: Rejection and failure mean that I am a less worthwhile person.

Rejection and failure can easily nudge us off the platform of truth into Error 1: *Because someone has rejected me or because I have failed, I am less worthwhile as a person.*

It is also possible to slip from the platform of truth into error on the other side. The truth that "Christ is all I need" may sometimes degenerate into a defensive posture to avoid personal hurt by maintaining a safe emotional distance in relationships. I once heard a lonely but proud man say to a Christian colleague, "Because I have Jesus, I am worthwhile with or without you. Your criticism therefore doesn't get to me at all. Nor does your acceptance really matter to me. It would represent a lack of faith in the Lord to let you affect me emotionally." He fell headlong into Error 2: *Hiding behind the truth of our worth in Christ to avoid feeling pain in relationships.*

Regardless of our spiritual maturity, we will acutely feel the pain of loss and rejection. And rightly so. Although our central relationship is with the Lord, we should enter into relationships with others deep enough to cause profound hurt when they fail. To say that Christ is sufficient does *not* imply that He is to function as some sort of asbestos cover protecting us from the pain of interpersonal fire. Rather, His resources make it possible for us to continue responding biblically in spite of the great pain we may feel, because the hurt, though great, will never be enough to rob us of our security and significance. And all we need to live as Christians, no matter what our circumstances, is the security of His love and the significance of participation in His purpose. We must never claim that our relationships with others do not affect us deeply: they do. But Christ's resources are enough to keep us going.

We can now complete the diagram.

In Christ, I am significant and secure; therefore I can live responsibly before God no matter what happens.

PLATFORM OF TRUTH

Error 1: Rejection and failure mean that I am a less worthwhile person.

Error 2: Christ is all I need; therefore I can avoid intimate relationships with others.

In the rest of this chapter we will think through how a Christian couple can become spiritually one by remaining atop the platform of truth.

Consider first how we can avoid falling into Error 1.

What are Christian husbands and wives to do when they keenly feel the insensitivity or disrespect of their spouses? How can they handle the acute pain of felt insecurity or insignificance that seeks relief behind the protective layers of emotional distance? How can a spouse who *feels* hurt realistically hang onto the truth of personal worth in Christ and thus avoid falling into the first error?

A woman I was counseling came to realize that for years she had been turning to her children for emotional fulfillment. Her husband had shut her out of his life, leaving her hungry for affection and loving response. She found what she wanted in her children. This led to a stubborn reluctance to approach her husband with love and warmth, and the source of her reluctance was a profound fear that he would react coldly to her overtures.

I suggested that she was depending on her husband to meet her personal needs and that her relationship was essentially selfish and manipulative. She shook her head and answered, "I know God is supposed to meet my need for love, but what am I supposed to do with all this hurt and fear? I believe God loves me, but I can't get it to really work inside me."

I recommended that she follow three steps to help her find solid footing on the platform of the truth that because Christ loves her, she can be obedient to all that Scripture commands.

Step 1: Fully acknowledge all your feelings to God.

Christians are often trained to pretend that they feel joyful and happy when they are really miserable. Because we "shouldn't" feel unhappy, we pretend we don't. Yet Hebrews 4:15 teaches that our Great High Priest can sympathize with us when we experience weakness. How wrong it is, then, to hide our emotional weaknesses from Him and to deny ourselves the comfort of noncritical understanding.

I encouraged this woman to fully acknowledge her hurt and pain before God, to literally and openly express what she was feeling in God's presence. So often people respond to such advice by reciting in contrite tones a prayer like "Lord, please forgive me for feeling hurt." But this misses the point entirely. We are not to pretend that we feel *penitent* when we feel *hurt*. When our stomachs churn with grief or anger or pain, we must humbly acknowledge to the One-who-sees-everything whatever we really feel. My client eventually prayed like this: "Lord, right now I am hurting more than I think I can endure. I feel like screaming, running away, hitting somebody! I don't want to feel this way, but I do. I feel worthless, empty, sad, and angry. Thank you for loving me exactly as I am."

Step 2: Reaffirm the truth of your security and significance in Christ.

One of the central truths of the Christian life is that our feelings need never determine how we believe or what we do. I exhorted this woman to remind herself that in Christ she is a fully loved and worthwhile woman despite her husband's rejection. To grasp this truth better, I asked her to picture her mind as a tape recorder. We observed that whenever her husband in some form rejected her, she immediately "played a tape" that said, "When my husband rejects me, my need for love cannot be met. I am dependent on my husband to make me feel loved."

The belief that Christ is not sufficient for our personal needs is a lie of Satan. I wrote a new "tape" on a card and asked her to play it (to repeat it to herself) the next time she perceived rejection from her husband. The new tape read: "My husband may reject me. If he does, I will hurt, perhaps a lot. But no matter how he treats me, I am at this moment totally and wonderfully loved by Christ. Because of His love, I am a secure woman."

Step 3: Commit yourself to ministering to your spouse's needs, knowing that however he may respond can never rob you of your worth as a person.

Because faith (playing the right tapes) is dead without works, the final step in helping my client to stand on the platform of truth was to encourage her to live out the implications of her new tape. Because she really is secure in Christ, she can make herself vulnerable to her husband's rejection by giving herself fully to him. The fact that she has not done so is sin and must be confessed as such. Repentance must follow.

I asked her to picture a cliff. In her imagination she was to see herself standing on its edge looking down into the abyss. The abyss represents what she fears would destroy her: her husband's rejection. While she remains on the cliff, she is safe; she cannot experience the deep pain of her husband's rejection so long as she keeps her distance from him. Every time she backs away from him or

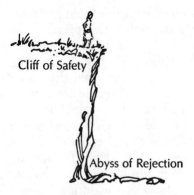

lashes out at him or hides behind a protective layer, she is choosing to remain on the cliff of emotional safety.

We discussed the biblical model of marriage that requires her to give herself fully to her husband for the purpose of helping him feel valuable and important. To obey the Lord, she would need to jump off the cliff of safety and distance into her husband's rejecting arms. She looked at me with terror in her eyes: "If I give myself to him I'll get hurt again. And I just can't handle any more rejection!"

I then asked her to visualize a strong rope tied securely around her waist, a rope that represents God's love and is held by the Lord from His position directly over the abyss. As long as she remains on the cliff, the rope hangs limply, because it is not challenged by her weight. The cliff, not the rope, is supporting her.

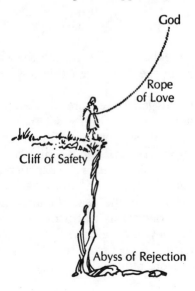

It was apparent to my client that from her position on the cliff she could never *feel* the strength of the rope. To develop the conviction that "Christ's love really does make me secure," she would have to jump, to leave the cliff of safety by committing herself to meeting her husband's needs no matter what the cost. She cannot meaningfully claim that she is trusting the Lord for all her needs until she leaps from the cliff. Until she is dangling over the abyss of rejection, held only by the love of God—and not until then—will she deeply know that Christ can meet her need for security. Her fear of rejection keeps her on the cliff. "Perfect love drives out fear" (1 John 4:18). But we will never know that love until we depend on it to preserve us from destruction.

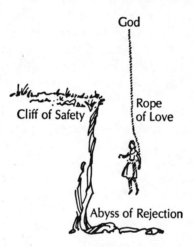

My client studied the diagram. "I can really see what you mean. But it doesn't take away the fear. Even thinking about making that jump terrifies me."

Her comment triggered one more addition to the sketch. After a fearful person jumps from the cliff of safety, there is an *interval of time* before the rope of love extends fully to support the person's weight over the abyss. The situation is similar to skydiving. When a skydiver steps from the plane, he or she experiences a few moments of sheer, unsupported falling until the parachute opens. For the scared Christian who makes the "leap of faith," the moments before Christ's love is experienced as real personal security may last an hour, a day, a week, a year, or longer. During this interval between the jump and the felt reality of security in Christ, the Christian will likely sense a fear more profound than any known before. At this time, relying on the Word of God is absolutely indispensable. "Underneath are the everlasting arms" (Deut. 33:27). "My flesh and my heart may fail, but God is the strength of my heart" (Ps. 73:26).

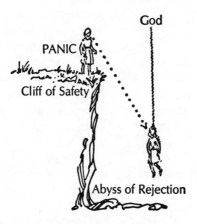

Let me summarize. When times of testing lead us into fierce personal struggles to maintain a sense of our worth as persons, it is easy to lose sight of the basis of our worth. To avoid the error of regarding ourselves as less worthwhile because of rejection or failure, we must—

Step 1: Openly acknowledge our painful feelings of hurt and worthlessness before the Lord;

Step 2: Reaffirm and continually remind ourselves of the truth that in Christ our security and significance are eternally intact;

Step 3: Act on the basis of this truth by squarely facing whatever we fear (rejection, failure, looking foolish, disapproval, etc.), depending on the strong love of God to conquer our fears.

THE PROBLEM OF EMOTIONAL WITHDRAWAL

Now consider how we can keep from slipping into Error 2. Falling from the platform into the second error ("Since Christ is all I need, I can withdraw from you emotionally") will destroy any hope of developing Spirit Oneness. Although it is true that our needs are fully met in Christ, it is also true that the Lord normally uses husbands and wives as His instruments to develop within each other a conscious awareness of personal worth. It is Christ alone who grants us security and significance, but it is often (by no means always) our spouses who help us to *feel* worthwhile.

God commands husbands and wives to submit to one another, that is, to put each other's *needs* first. I am to touch my spouse's deepest needs in such a way that I produce in her a conscious taste of what it is like to be deeply loved and respected.

Now, if we are to do our jobs well, we must explore how our behavior affects each other's awareness of our security and significance in Christ. In doing so, we will necessarily expose very private aspects of our personality. Nothing gives me a deeper sense of oneness with my wife than to share with her some of my struggles—the disappointments, hurts, fears, and unmet longings.

To know that she is aware of my most central struggles initially creates an incredible fear: I stand exposed and naked before her. Will she pass off my concerns lightly? Will she lose respect for me? Will she laugh or criticize? If she does reject me, I must depend on Christ's love as my basis for a sense of worth. But when she listens to me—really listens—and accepts me with my problems and frustrations, a closeness develops between us that can help me to regain the perspective to believe that I really am worthwhile in Christ. The kind of closeness that results from revealing to my wife central parts within me which I share with no one else is a central element in Spirit Oneness.

To remain atop the platform and to develop this kind of oneness, husbands and wives need to regard problems, not as a cause to withdraw, but rather as an opportunity to learn how to minister better to each other. Let me illustrate this truth with a personal example.

Some weeks ago, as my wife and I got into our car after a Bible study, she said in a voice mixed with anger and pain, "I really felt hurt tonight when you said . . . and now I'm so furious I can't even talk about it."

Exactly how does a person move from that beginning toward spiritual oneness? Consider a few of my options and select the one that you think would best develop closeness.

1. I could have ignored her, knowing that by morning she would settle down and speak politely and perhaps by the next evening become warm again. Why discuss a subject that will just develop into an argument and make matters worse? After all, regardless of whether I failed her or not, I am still accepted by Christ.

2. I could defend myself: "Whatever I did, I didn't mean to hurt you." Or I could attack her: "Well, you hurt me, too" or "You are really sensitive. You ought to trust the Lord more" or "All right, tell me what you're mad about now."

3. I could attempt to cut short an anticipated painful conversation with a quick apology.

If you selected any of these options as good bets to improve your marriage, you need this book.

Regretfully, although I know better, I chose to respond with the second option of defense and attack. The conversation went something like this:

> *Me:* "What on earth did I do now?" (Subtle attack on her oversensitivity)
>
> *Her:* "You put me down in front of the whole group when you said . . ."
>
> *Me:* "Honey, that was not a put-down! You completely misunderstood what I meant!" (Defend and attack)
>
> *Silence for three seconds*
>
> *Her:* "Well, it really hurt and I'm feeling mad!"
>
> *Me:* "OK, I'm sorry! What else can I say?" (A shift to Option 3: the conversation-ending apology)
>
> *Silence for thirty minutes*

During the second, longer silence, I became acutely aware that I had somewhere missed the road to Spirit Oneness. My wife and I were not experiencing a deep sense of our worth in Christ that enabled us to be mutually and sensitively responsive to each other's needs. I reflected on the fact that I really am a worthwhile person because of the Lord's love and purposes for me, whether or not I have been a success as a husband, and that my worth in Christ should be expressed not in retreat, but in an effort to minister to my wife. I approached her again, this time with a *different goal.* Before, I wanted to avoid pain by defending myself; now I determined to understand better what had happened and how I had hurt her in order to love her better in the future. Our second interchange went as follows:

> *Me:* "Honey, I really hurt you tonight. I guess I don't understand why what I said was so painful—but I want to. Will you talk to me about it?"
>
> *Her:* "I'm not sure I can. It still hurts a lot."
>
> *Me:* "I can accept that. I want to do a better job of making you feel loved. I failed you badly tonight, and I want to learn from it."
>
> *Her:* "I know you love me and are committed to making me feel good—but sometimes you seem so insensitive. I guess I really need to feel . . ."

And we talked for nearly an hour about our deepest needs and how we can be used of God to touch each other with healing rather than hurt. As we did so, we moved toward Spirit Oneness, the kind of profound closeness that results from meeting at the level of deepest needs.

CONCLUSION

Let us summarize the main points of the chapter:

1. We all have deep personal needs for security and significance that cannot be met outside of a relationship.
2. Many people deal with their needs wrongly by—
   a. Ignoring their existence and looking for satisfaction of *personal* needs with *physical* pleasures;
   b. Settling for counterfeit personal satisfaction through achievement, recognition, affluence, and the like which can never provide real security or significance;
   c. Turning to their marriage partners for security and significance. The result is a manipulative relationship designed to use each other for personal satisfactions. Because no marital partner is fully adequate to meet another's personal needs, such an exploitative relationship will inevitably experience conflict.
3. Only Christ can meet our needs, that is, provide us with eternal security and legitimate significance. We therefore must depend on Him to give us what our personal natures require.
4. It is difficult for us to grasp deeply the reality of our worth in Christ. To become subjectively and convincingly aware of our security and significance in Christ, we must—
   a. Trust His love enough to give ourselves fully to our spouses in an effort to minister to their needs and choose to continue our efforts to minister regardless of our spouses' response to us;
   b. Honestly explore the impact we make on each other's experience of self-acceptance as worthwhile persons.

Spirit Oneness can be defined as a relationship between husband and wife in which both partners—

1. Turn individually to the Lord in complete dependence upon Him for the satisfaction of their personal needs, and
2. Turn to each other in mutual commitment to—
   a. Give themselves to one another to be used according to God's purposes in each other's lives, and
   b. Openly explore the impact they make on one another's subjective experience of security and significance.

3
SOUL ONENESS:
I – Manipulation
or Ministry?

A pastor and his wife were approached by the elders of the church with a matter of deep concern. For nearly a year, undercurrents of dissatisfaction with the pastor's effectiveness had been rippling through the congregation. Clearly, something was wrong, but no one could pinpoint the difficulty. During recent months, however, a disturbing consensus was emerging among the church's leaders that the problems were somehow related to the pastor's marriage.

When the elders met to think through the situation, they agreed that the pastor's wife had been more and more consumed by her ministry of counseling troubled teen-agers. They wondered if perhaps this ministry so drained her energy that little was left for her ministry as a wife. It appeared that the more her counseling ministry grew, the more her husband had crowded his schedule with meetings, administrative duties, and routine responsibilities. The net effect seemed to be that he was losing the vital contact with people that he needed to serve the church effectively.

Although no one understood precisely how the pastor's retreat from his shepherding role related to his wife's preoccupation with counseling, the elders agreed that something in the marriage warranted attention. When they expressed their concerns to the couple at a special meeting, both reacted with chagrin and indignation. There were some tense moments, and firm exhortation was required before they would agree to seek counsel.

A few weeks later they entered my office, extending warm greetings to try to disguise their nervousness. I began by telling them that the elders had written me a letter stating their observations and concerns. The pastor vehemently stated his disagreement with the elders' conjectures and assured me that his marriage was as solid as ever and very much Christ-centered. His wife affirmed that she deeply loved her husband and had always put the home before her other ministries.

Our conversation revealed that this couple sincerely felt that they loved the Lord. They both evidenced strong knowledge of Christ's unconditional love as the basis of security and Christ's eternal purposes as the framework within which to find significance. Yet, though their hold on the truth went far beyond mere assent, I sensed that something important was missing. There was no spark of closeness between them, no spontaneity, no shared warmth, at best a stiff and well-protected friendliness.

In counseling, I usually encourage husband and wife to discuss specific recent events in their lives so that I can observe patterns of interaction. The pastor described a recent occasion when the couple enjoyed a rare evening out at a favorite restaurant. While they dined, his wife was called away to counsel a runaway girl who had just been picked up by the police. I asked the pastor how he felt as his wife left the table to deal with the emergency.

He smiled and answered, "She really has a heart for those kids. God has given her a unique and important ministry."

I continued, "I wonder if you ever wish that she would just relax with you during an evening without doing something related to her ministry and give you her full and undivided attention?"

"Oh, I suppose," he replied. "But I believe that what she does is truly important. And we've both dedicated our lives to whatever service God has for us."

At this point the wife fretted, "I don't agree with what I think you're getting at. My husband is more important to me than anything or anyone else except for God and His work. I happen to believe that God made us into a team who can minister to others. My husband pastors the church, and I offer what help I can to the kids God brings me. For the life of me, I can't see what is wrong with that."

Do this couple have a problem, or don't they? Does their marriage fit into God's design for oneness? They appear to understand that their needs are met in God, and they are dedicated to His service. Yet the relationship between them seems to be out of focus. What's wrong?

THE CONCEPT OF SOUL ONENESS

Many evangelical couples can more or less articulate the essential thinking involved in Spirit Oneness: Christ is all I need for security and significance; therefore I don't need to depend on my spouse to meet my needs, and I can devote my life to sacrificial giving, believing that the Lord will replenish my resources when they run dry. Some couples understand that because of God's promises, they can jump from the Cliff of Safety into the Abyss of Rejection, counting only on the Rope of the Love of Christ to protect them when others let them down.

But for probably a majority of Christians, these truths are academic. Too often, couples have not actively thought through the radical implications of these concepts for the marital relationship. And because they do not translate them from theory into experience, these truths never become vital. The only truths that eventually grip a Christian at the core of his being are the truths by which he consistently lives.

The concepts behind Spirit Oneness lead naturally and necessarily into a style of husband-wife relating that I call "Soul Oneness."

When the Bible speaks of people exercising their capacity to relate to God, it often refers to them as *spirits* or it talks about the *spiritual* nature of mankind (e.g., see John 4:24). But ". . . when the word soul is used to refer to the non-material being of man, it generally designates the man in some relationship to earthly circumstances."[1]

In explaining Spirit Oneness, my primary focus is on each partner's individual relationship to God and on how that spiritual relationship reaches into a person's needs for security and significance. But when our attention shifts to husbands and wives relating to each other, the term *Soul Oneness* seems an appropriate conceptual label.

As I understand God's design, the Spirit Oneness that couples can enjoy is intended to lead to a further interpersonal (or soul) oneness. This oneness grows from a *mutual, intelligent, and unreserved commitment to be an instrument of God to deeply touch a spouse's personal needs in a unique, powerful, and meaningful way.* Or, more simply, if the foundation of Spirit Oneness is mutual dependence on the Lord for personal needs, then the foundation of Soul Oneness is a mutual commitment to minister to one another's personal needs.

Like so many Christian couples, the pastor and his wife had no

---

[1] J. Oliver Buswell, *A Systematic Theology of the Christian Religion* (Grand Rapids: Zondervan, 1972), part II, pp. 239-40.

clear understanding of a relationship of mutual ministry. In fact, careful analysis revealed that their marriage was built on a primary commitment, not to minister to each other, but rather to maneuver themselves into a relationship of minimum emotional pain. Neither partner had any substantial awareness of either (1) the profound needs hidden beneath the other's spiritually acceptable facade, or (2) their incredible potential and opportunity for powerfully ministering to those deep needs.

There was a barrier between the couple that effectively blocked meaningful touching. The wall functioned much like a glass window between two people wanting to kiss: all of the proper motions were there, but none of the excitement—just cold glass. Only a deliberate shift from the subtle *commitment to manipulate* to the deliberate *commitment to minister* will shatter that barrier and permit the rich, intimate, fulfilling relationship of Soul Oneness. Let us see what this means.

WHAT IS YOUR REAL GOAL?

Everything we do has a goal. We are not conditioned animals that act automatically and unthinkingly in a programed response. Neither are we the hapless victims of internal, psychological forces that drive us relentlessly in unwanted directions. Although it may often *feel* as though we do things we don't want to do, the truth is that everything we do represents an effort to reach a goal that somehow, perhaps at an unconscious level, makes good sense to us.

Imbedded in our make-up are certain beliefs about how to become worthwhile or how to avoid injury to our self-esteem, how to be happy or how to avoid pain. As children, we acquire ideas about life from observing our parents (what makes them happy, why they feel bad), our teachers, television, and the like.

Because Satan is the prince of this world and because our fallen nature is naturally attracted to life plans that disregard God, each of us reliably develops *wrong beliefs* about how to find the meaning and love we need. And a belief about what I need implies a goal that I should pursue. If I *believe* I need food to live, I will make it my *goal* to get to the grocery store. *Beliefs determine goals.*

Suppose a boy is reared by parents who neglect him to pursue their own interests. He may develop the belief that there is no one who will attend to his needs. That wrong belief may lead him to strive for *absolute self-reliance* as the goal he must achieve to avoid personal pain.

The effect of childhood traumas is to teach wrong beliefs that are remarkably stubborn. Consider what happens as a girl watches her mother cry because her daddy doesn't come home at night. This unfortunate girl may learn the belief that men hurt women. She may then (unconsciously) set for herself the goal of never becoming emotionally vulnerable to a man. When she marries, her goal will motivate her to keep her distance, never to relax in her husband's love, never to give herself freely to him.

A boy whose father is preoccupied with business success would likely learn the belief that the way to feel good (or, to regard oneself as significant) is to "make it big."[2] His goal then becomes to gain prestige and position. When he falls in love, his sinful goal will motivate him to choose a woman who will be an asset in his climb to the top.

Let us review my thinking thus far:

1. We develop wrong *beliefs* about how to become secure and significant (or to avoid insecurity and insignificance).

2. These beliefs suggest a *goal*, which then motivates us to do what we do. This goal becomes a life principle around which we organize our efforts.

3. The best way to understand why we do what we do is to ask, "What are we trying to accomplish or avoid?" or "What is our goal?" When we determine what our goals are, we can identify and challenge the wrong beliefs behind the goals.

Note how this concept of goals relates to marriage. Consider the following situations:

> *Situation 1:* After the children are in bed, a husband rests his hand on his wife's thigh and says, "Honey, you're really gorgeous, and I love you."
>
> *Situation 2:* As her husband leaves the dinner table and begins stuffing his briefcase full of business papers, the wife asks, "Do you have to go back to the office again tonight?"
>
> *Situation 3:* After a long day with three young children, mother impatiently snaps at the oldest for failing to do an assigned chore. Dad looks up from behind his newspaper and says, "Honey, jumping all over him isn't going to help!"

Suppose I were to ask each speaker in these vignettes to state the *goal* or purpose of his or her comment. The romantic husband in Situation 1 might say, "To let my wife know I love her." The disappointed wife in Situation 2 might offer, "I just want him to be

---

[2]Perhaps ". . . the sins of the father are passed on to the third and fourth generation" (Exod. 34:6-7) as parents teach through their example wrong beliefs about how to become significant.

more a part of our family." And the helpful husband in Situation 3 would likely suggest, "I want to give her some perspective on what she's doing. I regard it as part of my role as spiritual leader to help her do the best job she can as wife and mother."

As we attempt to specify the motivation that should characterize our interactions with our mates, we should remember that we will fail to see the point clearly and to make needed personal application without the Holy Spirit's help. The deceitfulness of our hearts renders us incapable of accurately identifying our real goals without supernatural help.

In its fallen state the human consciousness is a marvelous instrument of self-deception. It is capable of selectively attending to only those motives that preserve our cherished image of ourselves as good and kind and of disowning or at least disguising the ugly, self-centered objectives to which we are really committed. Only the Spirit of God unfolding His truth as revealed in Scripture can cut through our lying hearts to expose our selfish motivation. Therefore we must continually open ourselves to His enlightening work, or we will miss the entire purpose of this chapter: to uncover the hidden and destructive objectives that guide the interactions of so many couples.

Think about the three vignettes. In Situation 1, the amorous husband may be communicating a message obvious to his wife: "I want sex." If he were to be told this, he might defend his goal as sanctioned by Paul's instructions to married couples not to defraud one another sexually (1 Cor. 7:1-5). Perhaps he would appeal to his legitimate desire for a supportive, affectionate wife. When stripped to the core, however, his goal is to manipulate his wife to respond to him in a way that *he* desires, with little or at best secondary concern for *her* need to feel loved and appreciated rather than pressured and used.

One husband responded to this idea, "But my wife has no reason to feel rejected or unloved. I *do* love her! I just want her to be more affectionate. Is that so wrong?"

Clearly, there is nothing wrong and everything right with a warm, sensual, physical relationship. There is nothing wrong with desiring sex and hoping for a responsive wife—and making his desire known to his wife. But to be *primarily motivated* by the goal of winning a response from one's spouse that is designed to satisfy one's own desires, however legitimate those desires may be, is a violation of love and therefore wrong. Love is essentially defined in terms of preoccupation with the *other's* needs. The central goal of every interchange between partners must be to minister to the other's deepest needs for security and significance. I may legitimately *desire* a particular response from my wife. But if my spouse for whatever reason fails to respond as I wish, then I must honor my goal of ministry through an uncomplaining, nonpressuring acceptance of my disappointing spouse. This acceptance would be motivated by my awareness of her deep needs for love and by my commitment to do all that I can do to touch those needs.

When a husband replaces the goal of ministry on behalf of the other with the goal of manipulation on behalf of oneself, he is guilty of a serious misrepresentation of Christ's love for His bride.

Consider Situation 2. When the wife softly inquires, "Do you have to go back to work again tonight?" what do you think is her real goal? Her not-so-hidden purpose is to somehow persuade her husband to remain at home. As she pursues this objective, notice that her essential focus is not on her husband's need for respect and acceptance, but rather on her desire that he satisfy her longings.

"But," she retorts to the confronting counselor, "he is rarely at home with the kids. They miss him terribly and have told me so! Don't you agree that a father should spend time with his attention-starved kids? Isn't that a part of his Christian responsibility?"

The answer, of course, is Yes. But her comment misses the point. The issue for the wife to consider is not "What should my husband do?" but rather "What should be my primary goal as I interact with him?" Her central purpose when she asks her husband to stay home is far more than to express her longings; this woman's real goal is to manipulate her husband to do what she believes he should. My concern lies with her motivation and not the rightness of the response she wants from her husband. In her efforts to persuade him to do what she thinks best, there is no thought of sacrificial ministry to his need for a sense of adequacy and respect. Her motivation, therefore, is wrong and her actions will move the marriage further away from Soul Oneness.

The husband in Situation 3 who reprimands his wife for speaking harshly to their child seems aware only of his wife's *error* and is inattentive to her *needs*. His goal apparently was to correct her error, not to minister to her. If we had tape-recorded his brain as he listened to his wife scold their youngster, it is unlikely that the tape would have picked up words like "I think my wife is handling our child incorrectly, but I want to be careful that I communicate neither rejection nor criticism to my wife. Above all else, I want her to know that I love her."

Because he did not have the conscious intention to minister, his real goal was to communicate his displeasure to his wife in the hope that she would speak more kindly to the child. Whenever the goal of our behavior is essentially to change the other person—whether the change is good or bad—we are wrong. Unless there is the purpose of communicating love based on an awareness of our spouses' needs, we qualify as manipulators, not ministers. *The key to achieving Soul Oneness is to maintain the fundamental goal of ministry to our partner's deepest needs and to keep that goal inviolate.*

THE PRINCIPLE OF MINISTRY

Paul instructs us in Ephesians 4:29: "Do not let any unwholesome talk come out of your mouths, but only what is helpful for [or consistent with the goal of] building others up according to their needs, that it may benefit those who listen."

The word translated "unwholesome" signifies something worthless that rots and decays. Paul is contrasting worthless words with words that last because they have a clear purpose: to meet the needs of others.

I believe Paul lays down here a core principle of relating that must govern interaction between all Christians. Certainly this principle applies to those who live together in the intimacy of marriage. I am to say nothing that in any way compromises the basic goal of ministering to the needs of the one to whom I am speaking. When I utter words with the *goal* of changing the other person without primary and conscious concern for his or her welfare, then those words are worthless. They serve no eternal purpose and will decay.

In marriage, words that do not comfortably fit within a commitment to minister are foreign to God's design and will not yield the dividends of increasing Soul Oneness. The romantic husband may persuade his wife to have sex; the unhappy wife may convince her husband to stay home; the rebuking husband may pressure his wife into never raising her voice toward the children in his presence—but the gain will not be toward oneness. There will be a change, and the change may appear to be an improvement, but the longed-for sense of intimate closeness will not develop.

Let me now state more fully the principle of ministry on which Soul Oneness depends:

> Husbands and wives are to regard marriage as an opportunity to minister in a unique and special way to another human being, to be

used of God to bring their spouses into a more satisfying appreciation of their worth as persons who are secure and significant in Jesus Christ.

Notice an essential point in this principle: It is Christ who provides us with security and significance. My love for my wife does not in the slightest degree add to the reality that she is thoroughly and eternally secure in Christ's love. Nor does my failure to love her as I should diminish the fact of her security. But my tangible, touchable, physically present love can bring to my wife a *deeper, experienced awareness of what it means to be loved.* I cannot add to the *fact* of her security, but I can add to her *feelings* of security.

Similarly, my wife's submissive respect for me does not increase my significance as a servant of Christ, but it does enrich my awareness of the adequacy that the Lord has already granted. The situation is much like a man who discovers that there is oil beneath my property. He does not make me wealthy; I was rich before he found the oil, but it is not until he makes me aware of the oil that I experience my wealth. Husbands do not make wives secure; wives do not make husbands significant. Only Christ can do this. And He does so the moment a person places his or her trust in Him as Savior and Lord. But husbands and wives can help convince their partners of their value and bring them to fuller enjoyment of their riches in Christ.

The couples who develop substantial Soul Oneness grasp the excitment of the ministry of marriage. To be able to profoundly influence another human being in a way that promotes a fulfilling awareness of their wholeness in Christ is a thrilling opportunity. A sovereign God has selected me from among all the billions of men who have ever lived for a ministry to which He has called no one else: the ministry of loving my wife with the unique committed love of a husband. How sad to think of the responsibilities of husband or wife as mere obligation or duty!

THE PRINCIPLE OF MANIPULATION
(and How It Destroys Soul Oneness)

To understand better why the principle of ministry is the necessary foundation for developing rich marital oneness, consider an example of how its opposite (the principle of manipulation) can ruin a relationship.

Mary's parents were divorced when she was seven years old. After her father left home, he rarely visited Mary and showed little evidence of loving concern. Mary's mother never quite recovered from the divorce and, for most of Mary's growing-up years, was preoccupied with scraping together enough money to live and finding enough pleasure to make her life worth living. Understandably Mary never felt loved. She developed the belief that to find the happiness that eluded her mother, she needed to marry a strong, loving man who would involve himself deeply in her life. Beneath this need for love rumbled a quiet, nagging fear: "Will I ever find the love I need?" We may draw a circle to represent Mary as a personal being who at her core experiences profound fear. Let a minus sign denote her fearful insecurity.

MARY

Bob's dad was a highly successful lawyer who, in the way he spent his time, clearly evidenced that he valued prestige and position above all else. From Bob's youthful perspective, his dad's business position seemed to bring him a great deal of satisfaction. As Bob observed this, he formed the belief that a personally worthwhile existence depends on success. Through high school and college, Bob nursed a private fear that he might not be able to reach his goal of extraordinary financial and positional achievement. We may draw Bob's personal circle with a minus sign in the center to represent his fear that he might not be able to achieve his chosen goal.

BOB

Reflect on the psychological condition of these two people who would one day marry. Mary believed that security required relationship with a strong, faithful man quite unlike her father; her goal, therefore, became to find that man and to draw her security from him. Bob believed that significance would come from success.

but he was unsure of his ability to attain the success he thought he needed; his goal, therefore, was first to regard himself as adequate and then to pursue business achievement.

During their courtship, Mary delighted in Bob's attention, listened intently to every word he said, laughed convincingly at every joke, and expressed admiration for his many good traits. He appeared to Mary to be a strong, self-assured, motivated, and loving man.

Bob felt good around Mary and concluded therefore that he had fallen in love. But what Bob mistakenly called love was in fact nothing more than an attraction to a woman who strengthened his sense of adequacy.

Mary wrongly interpreted Bob's warm interest as genuine love and regarded him as a means to realize the security she had desired for so long and feared would never come. Her feelings of intimacy with Bob were based entirely on what she thought Bob would do for her and not based on expecting to make a positive impact on Bob's life.

Because each was looking to the other to provide for their personal needs, their tic-on-a-dog relationship could not develop Spirit Oneness. And because their motivations were self-centered, they missed the Principle of Ministry and were building their relationship on the Principle of Manipulation. Look at how manipulative motivation blocked the development of Soul Oneness.

Within the first few months of their marriage, Mary, like all brides, was hurt by her husband on several occasions. A specially prepared meal did not receive the expected praise; his negative attitude toward helping around the house seemed to demean her work; her desire just to be warmly held ended often, at Bob's insistence, in the bedroom; a scratched auto fender earned a withering comment. Each experience of hurt struck deeply into her personal circle, and her dormant fear of rejection revived: "Will this relationship bring me pain? I could not endure the disappointment of having my hopes for love so quickly dashed."

To quiet the growing fear, Mary wrapped herself in protective layers designed to avoid more hurt. She became increasingly preoccupied with her own needs and lacked any motivation to minister to Bob's needs. She began thinking: "If I can just get him to be a little more loving, or if I can manage to keep our relationship distant enough so his rejection won't hurt as much, then perhaps I can minimize the pain." And so her goal became to control the relationship in a way designed to meet or to protect her needs. The principle of manipulation was fully in gear. She then began to drop comments like "Honey, I wish you'd just hug me without always making it into a sexual thing" or "You don't appreciate me at all" or "You don't treat me the way you did before we married." Beneath these "honest expressions of her feelings" (the misguided and destructive core of many unspiritual attempts to build a relationship) lay the hidden but forceful purpose to avoid further hurt. Their marriage now looked like this:

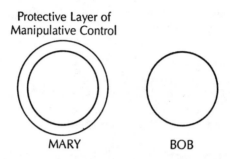

Shift the focus to Bob. His purpose in marrying Mary was also manipulative: he wanted to feel better about himself in order to promote the confidence he needed to succeed. When Mary started to communicate that he was not measuring up to her expectations, his feelings of adequacy weakened and his fear of never reaching his goal of success intensified. When people hurt, their immediate goal is to lessen the pain. So Bob began protecting himself from facing his feared inadequacy by retreating from Mary. His goal became to remove himself from the prospect of further hurt. Never once would his urgent attention to his own needs permit any real concern for Mary's needs; his fear consumed him. He too was operating according to the principle of manipulation.

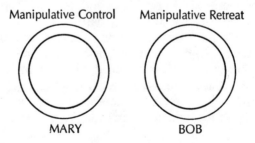

The vicious circle has begun: The more Bob retreats, the more Mary's fear of rejection increases. The more her fear increases, the more she attempts to manipulate Bob to protect herself. The more she tries to change him, the more she communicates that Bob is failing and the more his sense of inadequacy grows. The more inadequate he feels around Mary, the more he retreats. The more he retreats, the more her fear increases. The dreary cycle continues until two lonely people find themselves hopelessly trapped behind thick walls of their own making that keep them from ever really touching each other. The tragedy is that these people are not merely two misguided souls longing for intimacy; they are also self-centered people so committed to the principle of manipulation that their walls will likely remain in place until they divorce or die. Neither partner entertains the faintest thought of being used of God to meaningfully reduce the other's fear.

There is only one escape from this self-made prison, and that is to completely rebuild the relationship on a radically different premise. Both partners must change their goals from manipulation to ministry. And the revolution requires supernatural intervention. Otherwise it cannot succeed.[3]

CHANGING GOALS

The power of God is indispensable to altering one's commitments meaningfully. Until I am aware that my needs are already met in Christ, I will be motivated by emptiness to meet my needs. When by simple faith I accept Christ's shed blood as full payment for my sins, I am brought into a relationship with an infinite Being of love and purpose who fully satisfies my deepest needs for security and significance. Therefore I am freed from self-centered preoccupation with my own needs; they are met. It is now possible for me to give to others out of my fullness rather than needing to receive from others because of my emptiness. For the first time, I have the option of living selflessly.

Consider how this supernatural change in our goals can occur once the foundation of justification is in place. From a human perspective, three elements are required to shift from manipulation to ministry:

---

[3]Marriage counseling that does not concern itself fundamentally with changing the goals of husband and wife from manipulation to ministry and that fails to bring spiritual resources to bear in accomplishing this task amounts to nothing more than instruction in congenial manipulation.

> *Element 1.* A decisive and continuous willingness to adopt the commitment to minister;
> *Element 2.* A substantial awareness of your partner's needs;
> *Element 3.* A conviction that you are God's chosen instrument to touch those needs.

Element 1: A decision to minister

The commitment to minister does not evolve naturally. To develop the right motivation, more is required than time spent in the Bible, sincere prayer, and the study of good Christian literature. Although a consistent devotional life is necessary for the shift to be lasting and thorough, the path from manipulation to ministry centrally involves a deliberate choice, or better, a series of deliberate choices. Selfless motivation is not developed by passively "letting go and letting God." The Spirit of God quickens our mind and our wills, enabling us to repent and obey. First, I must agree with God that manipulation to meet my own needs is sinful. I must turn from my sin, believing that a good God leads me along good paths (repent). Then I must choose to walk along the path of ministry (obey).

All of us face various character-molding decisions every day. To speak with my spouse, I must consciously and deliberately *think:* "My purpose right now must be to help my wife realize her value as a person. What can I do that will accomplish this?" My insides may urgently scream with a compelling desire to defend myself, criticize her, or make other manipulative responses. Amid this inner turmoil, I must make a decision to do what will help her feel loved. As I make the choice, the Spirit of God provides the power to make it real—but I must make the choice.

The natural resistance to truly giving ourselves to the other is rooted in our stubborn fear that if we really give, with no manipulative purpose, we will be shortchanged. Our needs will not be met. At best we'll be disappointed; at worst, we'll be destroyed.

But God is faithful. We are to trust His perfect love to cast out our fear, believing that as we give to our spouses in His name, He will supernaturally bless us with an awareness of His presence. And He will. But it may take time—perhaps months—before we sense His work in us. The willingness to give unconditionally does not come by simply deciding to be selfless. The stain of self-centeredness requires many washings before it no longer controls our motivation. Many commitments to minister and much time spent with God will transpire before we know what it means to *give.*

Our job is to learn faithfulness and to press on in obedience, not giving in to discouragement or weariness, believing that God will always honor the conscious and persevering motivation to serve Him. When a spouse becomes more critical, drinks more heavily, or rejects efforts of ministry, we are to continue in our obedience, believing that our responsibility before God is to obey and to trust Him for the outcome.

Element 2: An awareness of your partner's needs

Think again of the pastor and his wife whose marriage was friendly but neither intimate nor rewarding. Much of my counseling involved encouraging each partner to become aware of his or her own aching needs and then expose those needs to the other.

I am convinced that most husbands and wives have little awareness of the intense yearnings crying from their partners' hearts. Too often, one of the protective layers people hide behind is the layer of "apparent togetherness" of "I can handle things" or "I'm O.K. and I assume you're O.K." Confident smiles coupled with spiritual platitudes about "all things working for good" often mask a deep longing to be accepted. We fervently desire someone to know us as we are—worried, shattered, scared, angry, lustful— and to accept us anyway.[4]

Therefore I regard an honest sharing of who I am with my spouse as consistent with the principle of ministry. I am not to complain about how bad I feel; rather, I am to remind myself that my needs are met in Christ and to share with my spouse how I feel in our relationship. My goal in sharing is to vulnerably reveal myself, legitimately desiring, but never demanding, a loving response.

Why was the pastor afraid to tell his wife how he really felt about her time-consuming ministry? He feared a response of indifference, surprise, or criticism. So what was his goal in *not* sharing his feelings? To protect himself from hurt. His own needs were his primary concern. He justified refusing to share his hurts by telling himself that he did not want to burden her or stand in the way of her important work with teens. But in fact, his root motivation was self-protective and manipulative. For him to shift to a ministry model of marriage, he needed to own up to his emotions and reveal them to his wife.

She too was out of touch with her fears. Years of denying her real longings for relationship and settling for the substitute satisfac-

---

[4]In our culture some folks make a fetish of displaying their miserable insides. Clearly, there are two extremes to be avoided: fearful hiding and indiscriminate exhibitionism.

tion of a valid ministry had made it very difficult for her to recognize her real needs. A few sessions of directive probing helped her to uncover some long-held hurts and well-nursed grudges. Another session was needed before she would express these feelings to her husband.

Exhortations to minister to our spouses mean little until we are aware that our spouses need our ministry. One husband put it well when he said, "My wife is so strong and self-sufficient that to offer her my love is like giving Rockefeller a nickel. She just doesn't need what I have to offer." Because many husband and wives see no evidence that their ministry can be meaningful to their partners, it is essential that they develop an awareness of their spouse's deepest needs. We can create a climate of noncritical acceptance to encourage our spouses to risk becoming vulnerable. If our partners will not open up, we must realize that because they are made in God's image, deep needs do exist, even if they are well hidden. We must pray for wisdom to know what to do to touch those needs.

Element 3: A conviction that you are God's chosen minister to your spouse

So many of us struggle with a sense of inadequacy and incompetence that it is difficult to believe that we have the resources to bear fruit in our ministry of marriage. Relationships are complicated. People are complicated. We may feel stupid, unable to figure out exactly what we should do: "No matter what I do, it makes no difference to her." "He is such a puzzle to me. I just don't know what to do when he gets like that. Everything I try flops."

Books have been written on principles of effective verbal interaction. I have read several. Yet I still find myself stumped sometimes when I face relationship problems that the principles do not seem to cover. Christians are called upon to believe that in spite of our confusion and incompetence, our sovereign God has made no mistake in assigning us the ministry of touching our spouses' deepest needs. Regardless of the circumstances under which people were married, God affords each married partner a unique opportunity to minister in a special way to his or her mate.

The pastor and his wife were overwhelmed as they learned of the other's needs. Neither felt adequate for the task of ministry presented to them. They feared that their efforts would fail and that they would prove terribly lacking in the resources needed to deepen their relationship. Yet the condition for effective ministry is utter reliance on God that grows out of a sense of our inadequacy for the task. Admitted weakness makes it possible for us to abide in Christ, trusting Him for fruit (John 15:1-8).

Now, with all three elements for change solidly in place, it is possible to begin to shift from manipulation to ministry. Consider an example of how it's done. Remember that unless we deliberately adopt the goal of ministry on a moment-by-moment basis, our natural, reflexive goal will generally be to manipulate our spouses for our advantage.

Fred enters his home after a long day at work. His automatic, unplanned, and perhaps unconscious goal likely involves a desirable response from his wife Joan, perhaps a friendly greeting, a warm hug, or a prepared dinner. Suppose she welcomes him by asking, "Why are you so late? You said you'd be home by six and it's nearly seven."

Joan has blocked Fred's goal. Reflect for a moment. How do people *feel* when their goal is blocked? Most often, they become angry or at least frustrated. Fred feels anger toward his wife. He admits to himself that he feels like retorting with a snappy comment like "Hey, thanks for the warm welcome! Sure is nice to come home!"

What should he do? His options are (1) to express his anger, (2) to defend his late arrival, (3) simply to ignore Joan's comment and wash up for dinner, or (4) to soothe her with a warm embrace. Remember the essential point of the chapter. Soul Oneness depends on our *motives* for what we do more than on the *specifics of what we do.* The question Fred needs to ask is not *"What should I do?"* but rather *"What is my goal?"*

Fred's anger should be a strong warning that his goal was manipulative. He was demanding a response from his wife that would meet his need of the moment. If Fred is (1) committed to the principle of ministry, (2) aware of his wife as a woman who longs to feel loved, and (3) convinced that he is God's instrument to tangibly represent Christ's love to his wife, then he is able to change his goal. The actual operation involves replacing thoughts like "Why can't she be pleasant when I come home?" to "My goal right now is to let my wife know that she is a loved and special woman."

Think again of the mind as a tape recorder. The automatic "tape" we play reflects our manipulative goal of changing our spouse: "Why can't she greet me warmly?" To change goals, we must decisively eject that wrong tape and insert a new one into position, that is, choose a new sentence to reflect our changed goal: "I want to make her feel loved."

Changing tapes must be more than a mechanical procedure. As we replace our selfish thoughts with giving intentions, we need to remind ourselves that we are freely choosing to minister because we believe God. Although our feelings may not immediately shift from anger to compassion, we can convey noncritical acceptance to our spouses if ministry is our freely selected purpose.

The crux of the matter is, Do we really want to accept the goal of ministry at this moment? The more we are willing to do so, the more surely our marriage will move toward satisfying levels of Soul Oneness.

SUMMARY

Spirit Oneness requires each partner to trust Christ for complete satisfaction of deep personal needs and to regard marriage as a unique experience of sharing life in Christ.

Soul Oneness is the mutually satisfying relationship that develops when each partner recognizes the opportunity that marriage provides. The route to Soul Oneness is helping our mates to appreciate more their fundamental worth as people who bear the image of God and saints who are truly secure and significant in Christ.

Soul Oneness is felt subjectively as a relationship so intimate that only sexual intercourse can fully express it. This sort of oneness can develop only when both partners accept an unconditional commitment to minister to the needs of the other, hoping for but never demanding reciprocal ministry.

Relationships built on manipulative efforts to enhance our own feelings of being loved or to protect ourselves against further hurt will never achieve the oneness God wants us to enjoy. A shift from the principle of manipulation to the principle of ministry is the only route to Soul Oneness.

4
SOUL ONENESS:
II – Communication, or "What Do I Do When I'm Angry?"

Most surveys of marital troubles list communication as one of the top contenders for the title of "most common problem." Couples often report things like—

- "We can't talk about anything important without getting into a fight."
- "Whenever I try to tell her how I feel, she seems disinterested and sometimes critical."
- "He simply avoids all conversation about us. We can discuss vacation plans, where to send the kids to school, and what car to buy, but he refuses to talk about our relationship."
- "She's too emotional. She's either crying or hollering or complaining about something. I just avoid her—it's easier."
- "We both try to talk through our problems, but it never makes us feel closer. We get defensive or impatient and end up farther apart than when we began. Something's wrong."

Many efforts to communicate fail to resolve problems and instead generate new frictions. Our purpose in this chapter is to think through principles for developing effective communication, the kind that moves people toward Soul Oneness.

We have established that the essential foundation for a biblical marriage relationship is an unqualified commitment to the goal of ministry. Each partner must be willing to minister to the needs of the other regardless of the response. Although all of us will fail to implement that commitment perfectly, our responsibility is to remind ourselves continually that our highest purpose as husbands or wives is to be an instrument for promoting our partners' spiritual and personal welfare. Because of our stubborn inclination to pursue manipulative goals and our remarkable ability to disguise them as worthy objectives, we must sustain a determined openness to God's Spirit convicting us whenever we unwittingly shift from ministry to manipulation.

This commitment to minister is not an option. We are not invited to "consider the possibility" of approaching our marriage this way. God explicitly instructs us to submit one to another (Eph. 5:21)—to submit to our wives' needs by loving them and to submit to our husbands' needs by respecting them. Too many evangelicals read these instructions, acknowledge them as their responsibility, then disregard them in married life.

Communication problems can usually be traced to a failure in the commitment to minister, or more simply, to wrong goals. This diagnosis is simple, but not simplistic. Psychologists tend to pursue the complexities surrounding a clear truth until the simplicity of the truth is lost. For example, workshops on communication teach verbal strategies for sharing and listening in nonattacking and non-defensive styles, but they rarely pinpoint the key problem of selfish motivation. Sharing and listening skills are important to learn, but I rather think that the effort spent teaching the skills could sometimes be better used to persuade people to stop living self-centered lives and to seek first the purposes of God. Even when communication teachers recognize the manipulation involved, they can effect no real shift to ministry without the resources of the gospel of Christ.

A biblical understanding of communication problems is neither simplistic nor irrelevant. The Book of James speaks about the problem with the keen insight of a divinely inspired diagnostician.

> What causes fights and quarrels among you? Don't they come from your desires that battle within you? You want something but don't get it. You kill and covet, but you cannot have what you want. You quarrel and fight. You do not have because you do not ask God. When you ask, you do not receive blessing because you ask with wrong motives (James 4:1-3).

The clear teaching of Scripture is that communication problems inevitably result whenever people pursue self-centered goals. Most of us enter marriage with the foolish but reasonable-sounding belief that we *need* (not desire or long for, but need) our spouses to respond to us a certain way if we are to be significant and secure. We must become convinced of the sufficiency of Christ to the point where our goals toward our spouses shift from manipulation to ministry.

This is all simple enough to comprehend as a workable model for marriage relationships. To put it into practice is quite another matter. No belief is more persistent than the one that says my partner must treat me a certain way. We can often find biblical support to justify our demand that our mates behave differently. And of course, we may be correct in believing that God would like our spouses to change. But it is very difficult to acknowledge that it is never my place to *demand* anything of my spouse, or to admit that my commitment to minister does not depend on my partner's attitudes or behavior. It requires mountain-moving faith to believe that Christ is sufficient for me and that I am capable of giving to my partner regardless of the pain of rejection.

The Bible regards faith as a growing quality. Maintaining the goal of ministry when our partners let us down demands a mature and well-nourished faith. Many Christians have not yet reached a level of spiritual development where their goals are consistently loving. I still get annoyed when my wife misses my cue for her to express appreciation for something I have done. And when I am annoyed (or hurt or discouraged), it is difficult to hold onto the proper goal of ministry. The fact that I am annoyed suggests that my goal was manipulative: I wanted my wife to notice me. More sanctifying work is needed for most of us to pursue the goal of ministry consistently.

But what are we to do in the meantime? Here we sit, imperfect Christians with frustrations and hurts and fears, unable to change our wrong goals fast enough or thoroughly enough to make all the negative emotions disappear. If we tell our mates how we feel, will that promote Soul Oneness or just produce more hurt? If we don't tell them how we feel, won't the held-in emotions create distance between us and drive us further away from the oneness we seek?

The negative feelings that all couples experience toward each other are a major obstacle to developing effective communication. Perhaps the question I hear most often when I lead marriage seminars is, What do I do with my feelings? Should we tell our spouses everything we feel? Is total openness a healthy, biblical value?

To develop the kind of communication that builds Soul Oneness, two elements are required:

1. A commitment to the goal of ministry;
2. A strategy for handling negative emotions that neither violates the goal of ministry nor creates distance between the partners.

Chapter 3 dealt with the first element. The rest of this chapter will consider the second.

WHAT DO I DO WITH MY FEELINGS?

It may appear from my emphasis on "ministry to the other" that I regard any sharing of negative emotions as a violation of the goal of ministry and therefore wrong. Many Christians apparently hold the view that expressing nonpositive emotions is always sinful. Instructions like "You should never be angry" or "If you can't say something nice, say nothing" reflect a position that binds people in the strait jacket of emotional denial. Spouses pretend they feel one way when they really feel quite different. The masks remain rigidly in place, glued on tightly by the belief that Christian relationships must always consist of accepting smiles and warm expressions of love. In fact, the masks serve to keep closed a Pandora's box of hidden hurt and anger.

Some secularists, blissfully unconcerned with biblical injunctions to put off malice and to be kind to one another, have reacted to the teaching of suppression by insisting that feelings are neither good nor bad, they just *are*. For them, the wisdom of expressing emotions is measured, not in moralistic terms, but by pragmatism: "Will I feel better if I express myself?" or "I have a right to assert myself by telling you how I feel. I will do so if I want to."[1]

Two options confront us: (1) we can *stuff* our feelings inside, recoiling from them with spiritual horror, or (2) we can assertively *dump* them on others, reminding ourselves as we get things off our chests that "I have a right to be me." As I understand the Bible, neither strategy is consistent with God's design for developing oneness through communication.

Recall the concept of the Platform of Truth in chapter 2. The biblical position on a given subject can often be represented as a narrow, slippery platform from which it is easy to fall to either side. This illustration depicts the two wrong ways of handling feelings.

---

[1]The book *Responsible Assertive Behavior* encourages expression of wants on the grounds that ". . . people have the right to 'want' and assume that others will respect their personal rights" (p. 64). They acknowledge, however, that "the question of the origin . . . of personal rights remains unresolved. Are any of these rights inalienable? Are they inherent simply because we are human? . . . At this stage, these fundamental issues are still unresolved for us" (p. 64). Here the authors essentially admit that they have no foundation for the central thesis of their book. A. J. Lange and P. Jakubowski, *Responsible Assertive Behavior* (Champaign, Ill.: Research Press, 1976).

HANDLING FEELINGS

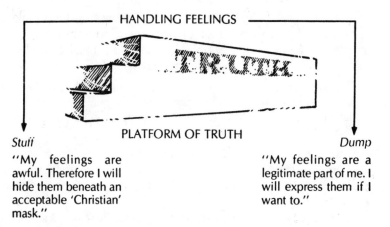

Stuff	PLATFORM OF TRUTH	Dump
"My feelings are awful. Therefore I will hide them beneath an acceptable 'Christian' mask."		"My feelings are a legitimate part of me. I will express them if I want to."

If we should neither hold in our feelings nor express them indiscriminately, exactly what are we supposed to do with them?

• When your husband embarrasses you in front of your friends, what are you to do with your anger?

• When your wife reacts to your idea in a condescending manner, what should you do with your irritation?

• When your husband disciplines the children too harshly because of his own frustrations, what are you supposed to do with your fear and fury?

• When your wife tells you she feels attracted to another man, how are you to handle your jealousy and hurt?

Consider specific forms of the two options:

Stuff: Remind yourself that God loves you and that it isn't necessary for your spouse to change. Then smile warmly and minister by asking, "What can I do to make you feel more special?"

Dump: Remind yourself that because God loves you, you are a worthwhile person who has a right to express your feelings. Tell your spouse exactly how you feel as a way of affirming your wholeness in Christ.

The first option will at best produce an anxious spiritual phony. Far too many well-meaning Christians clench their teeth and utter appropriate words to cover angry feelings. The hostility slowly builds until it erupts in either a fit of temper or a bad case of colitis.

The second option will likely avoid both psychosomatic stomach problems and outbursts of anger. But to share negative feelings with the goal of asserting your rights will neither edify your spouse nor reflect godly humility on your part.

For a biblical perspective we need to know how God looks at feelings. A suggestive account of one way God views emotional expression is recorded in Ezekiel 24. God told Ezekiel that He was about to take the life of his wife, a woman Ezekiel loved dearly.

> The word of the LORD came to me: "Son of man, with one blow I am about to take away from you the delight of your eyes. Yet do not lament or weep or shed any tears. Groan quietly; do not mourn for the dead . . ." (vv. 16-17).

Now, the death of a beloved wife is naturally an occasion for profound grief and sadness. But notice how God instructed Ezekiel to handle his feelings. In verse 17, God told His servant to "groan quietly."

Two truths stand out in these directions. *First*, God acknowledged that Ezekiel will feel real emotions. He did not tell Ezekiel to feel anything other than what he did feel. The fact is that we are incapable of directly changing an emotion. We have two sets of choices in responding to a feeling: (1) we can acknowledge them or pretend they do not exist, and (2) we can express or not express them. God's instruction to groan encourages Ezekiel to acknowledge how he feels, to experience inwardly the weight of a painful response to a pain-producing event.

Note that Ezekiel's feelings were not sinful. There are emotions that must be regarded as part of an unrighteous approach to a problem and can therefore be labeled as sinful. In an earlier book, I suggested that negative emotions which block out compassion may fairly be thought of as sinful and that negative emotions which are in no way inconsistent with compassion are not sinful.[2]

Both sinful emotions (e.g., jealousy, greed, lust) and nonsinful emotions (e.g., sorrow, grief, regret) need to be fully acknowledged before the Lord. But the attitude with which we acknowledge each kind of feeling should be different. When I experience a nonsinful but painful emotion, I am to come to the Lord fully expressing my feelings in humble dependence on His comfort and sufficiency. When I experience sinful emotions, however, I must approach Him with an attitude of contrition and repentance, trusting in His forgiveness and His promise to complete His work begun in me. Practically, this means I should openly experience my unrighteous feelings before God in a humble spirit of confession. This does not consist of superficial prayers like "Oh, Lord, please forgive me for being angry." Rather, it is better to cry, "God, I am *furious*! I am

---

[2] *Effective Biblical Counseling* (Grand Rapids: Zondervan, 1977).

livid with rage! And I know I am wrong! I want to go your way and be filled with your compassion, but right now I am bitter. Please forgive me! I commit myself to your purposes." I am emphasizing that we must never suppress any emotion, whether by denying its existence or by minimizing its fullness.

Second, God instructed Ezekiel to deny himself any form of public expression of his private grief. Ezekiel was to acknowledge inwardly how he felt ("groan"), but he was not to express this outwardly ("quietly"). Remember the two sets of choices that confront us in our emotions: we can acknowledge or ignore them, and we can express or not express them. Ezekiel was to acknowledge, but not express.

To psychologists who emphasize the need to work through painful emotions, such advice might warrant a malpractice suit. We are sometimes told that emotions—especially heavy ones like guilt and grief—require cathartic expression or they will build and cause psychological harm. On the other hand, people from the "deny emotions" camp who steadfastly refuse to admit when they feel negative emotions would also have problems with God's advice. In their minds, time spent getting in touch with feelings is wasteful and wrong. But God's instructions were clear: acknowledge, be in touch with how you feel, but don't express your feelings openly.

Succeeding verses in Ezekiel 24 reveal that God had a definite reason for instructing His prophet as He did. The absence of customs of mourning was intended to convey powerfully to an apostate nation that an impending judgment for their sin would be so severe that by comparison the death of a wife justified no tears at all.

In other words, after instructing Ezekiel to acknowledge his feelings inwardly, God directed him to control the expression of his emotions according to the constraints of a larger purpose. It seems to me that despite the special prophetic circumstances of Ezekiel's experience, a very helpful principle emerges from God's command to "groan quietly":

When an emotion arises within us, we are to—

1. Acknowledge to ourselves and to God how we feel, allowing ourselves to inwardly experience the full weight of our emotions;

2. Subordinate the public expression of our feelings to the goal of allowing God to use us for His purposes.

Thus, emotional *acknowledgment* is always proper; emotional *expression* is legitimate only when it does not conflict with our fulfilling God's purposes. I am never free just to get things off my chest (dumping). I must freely admit to myself and to God how I feel, confident that God's justifying grace provides me with His acceptance no matter what my emotions are. I am not to suppress my feelings. I must then evaluate whether expressing my acknowledged feelings to anyone other than God will serve His purpose and control their expression accordingly.

We can now define the biblical strategy for handling emotions that belongs on the Platform of Truth.

HANDLING EMOTIONS
Fully acknowledge inwardly; selectively express outwardly according to God's purpose.

Stuff

Dump

PLATFORM OF TRUTH

After we admit to ourselves that we feel angry or hurt, we must *immediately* determine to retain full control over which emotions we express and how we express them. I might add that there is no inherent incompatibility between controlled expression and spontaneous expression of emotions. We can cultivate control over our spontaneous reactions.

Once the principle of "first acknowledge, then selectively express" is established, our task is to figure out *when* expressing our emotions serves God's purpose of ministry to our spouses. To answer this difficult question adequately, we must first understand another concept: the difference between goal and desire.

GOAL VS. DESIRE

I have repeatedly talked of the essential *goal* of communication as ministry. But to suggest that husbands and wives can achieve good communication merely by choosing proper goals is unrealistic. No matter how resolutely we commit ourselves to the goal of ministering to our spouses, we will experience an unquenchable *desire* for our partners to minister to us.

When I feel discouraged, my wife's encouraging attitude and words mean more to me than I could express. A pastor-friend recently told me how much it means to him to come home at night to a loving wife; he desires her warmth so much it almost seems he could not live without it. Many women have told me how they cry out, from the very depths of their being, for a sensitive, accepting expression of love from their husbands. No matter how strong our commitment to minister and our dependence on Christ to meet all our needs, each of us longs for a certain kind of response from our mates. What are we to do with these yearnings? Are we to bury them beneath renewed commitments to minister? Must we pretend that because Christ is sufficient, it really doesn't matter how our spouses treat us?

God intended couples to live together in an intimate relationship of mutual impact: we are to feel keenly the effects of our spouses' attitudes and actions. It matters very much whether we are sacrificially loved and thoroughly accepted by our marriage partners. We feel hurt when our spouses reject us and we feel good when our spouses accept us, because we strongly desire their love. This desire is natural and good. It reflects the truth that we are not mere animals, but personal beings made in God's image, real people who have the ability to affect one another profoundly. Without this desire for each other's love, we would be incapable of receiving another person's acceptance with real joy. But—and this is a crucial point—*this desire must never become our goal.*

Let a circle represent our *need* for security and significance. Let an outer circle represent our legitimate *desire* for richly feeling security and significance in our relationships.

The central thesis of this book is that Christ is adequate to meet our needs fully. To put it differently, He is able to fill to capacity the inner circle in the sketch. He has never promised, however, to fill the outer circle of desire. Yet all our longings for warmth, kindness, understanding, respect, and faithfulness from our spouses are in that outer circle. We seem to *feel* significant and secure when these desires are met, but the Lord has not promised that He will grant these desires.

When these desires remain unmet, we feel valid and legitimate pain. Something good is missing. God has chosen our spouses as His special instruments for helping us to experience more fully what it means to be loved and important. When our *needs* are met, we *are* secure and significant. When our *desires* are met, we *feel* secure and significant. When our desires are not met, we hurt. But because our need to be a worthwhile person is met in Christ whether we feel it or not, we can choose to maintain the goal of ministering to a spouse who is failing to meet our desires.

Now I can define the terms I am using. *A goal is an objective that is under my control.* When reaching an objective depends solely on my willingness to do certain things, it may properly be called a goal. By this definition, ministry to one's spouse is a goal that a Christian can hope to reach better than others. The Christian is fully secure and significant in Christ whether he feels it or not and is capable of operating from fullness. He can give because he has something to give. The unbeliever's sense of security and significance does not have the same source, and what he or she gives has no real foundation. Because he is empty, the unbeliever cannot pursue the goal of ministry in a way that pleases God.

A desire is an objective that I may legitimately and fervently want, but cannot reach through my efforts alone. To fulfill a desire requires the uncertain cooperation of another. Wanting our husbands to be more reasonable in their discipline of the children is a *legitimate desire* but an *illegitimate goal.* Although a wife can influence her husband to treat the children more gently, she does not have the power to guarantee that he will change. She can perhaps alter the probabilities of his becoming more reasonable, but she cannot force him to behave differently. To make it her goal to change him, she presumes a power she does not have. When she chooses a goal to pursue, she must think in terms of *her response to him* rather than his response to anyone. His manner of handling the children must forever remain, for her, in the category of desire.

Whether we perceive our objective as a goal or a desire makes a great difference in what we do with it. My objective may be that it rain this afternoon. Because I cannot control whether it rains, that objective is a desire; therefore I will not engage in meaningless efforts to make it rain. We must never assume responsibility for fulfilling our desires. All we can do is pray that the One who is in control will allow our objectives to be realized. If I perceive my objective of rain as a goal, I will set about to find some way to make it happen; but because I do not have the ability to control whether it rains, I will only experience frustration and anger.

A legitimate goal, however, can be reached through my efforts. Therefore I am responsible to act in ways that will realize my purpose.

I may not feel like doing what is required to reach the goal, but I can do it if I choose. My lawn my be parched. I *desire* that it rain, but my *goal* is to see to it that my lawn receives water. I can choose to purchase a sprinkler with which to water the lawn. I may not want to drive to the store and spend the money but, assuming I have the time and the cash, I can choose to do so if I want to reach my goal.

The proper response to a desire, then, is *prayer*. To a goal, the appropriate response is a set of *responsible actions*. If we confuse our goals and desires, our responses will be wrong. Too many people pray for their goals ("Lord, make me treat my wife more kindly") and assume responsibility for their desires ("Honey, will you get off my back?"). The principle to remember is, *Pray for your desires and assume responsibility for your goals.*

Because it is both important and difficult to discern whether a given objective is a goal or desire, we should sharpen the distinction more.

Consider an objective something you want. If the objective is a desire, you will pray for it. If the objective is a goal, you will get busy and make it happen. To decide whether an objective is a goal or a desire, it will be helpful to ask two questions:

1. Exactly what is the objective? What do I want to see accomplished?

2. Can I by my own efforts, with cooperation from no one, control whether this objective is realized?

If the answer to question 2 is yes, then the objective is a legitimate goal and not a desire. If the answer is no, the objective should not be regarded as a goal, for which you assume responsibility; it is rather a desire, for which you pray.

Think about the following examples. Each statement represents an answer to the first question, What is the objective? Determine whether each objective is a goal or desire by asking the second question: Can I control whether this objective is fulfilled?

1. I want my husband to understand how I feel.
2. I wish I could get through to my wife that I do love her. She is so insecure.
3. I'd come back to my husband if he were more loving.
4. I really want to feel more sexually attracted to my husband. I just don't feel any desire for sex.
5. I need to make more money this year so I can better provide for my family.
6. I want God to use my wife and me to reach at least one of our neighbors with the gospel this year.

Each of these objectives is a desire, not a goal. In no case can an individual by his or her own efforts guarantee that the objective will be fulfilled.

In the next group of sentences, the objective of each of the previous six examples has been changed from a desire to a goal.

1. I will write my husband a letter telling him how I feel. I hope he understands (*desires*), but my objective is to express myself as clearly as I can (*goal*).
2. My wife is so insecure. Although I can't be sure that she will feel loved (*desire*), I will list five things I can do this week that I believe would reflect my love for her, and then I will do them (*goal*).
3. I'm scared to death to come back to my husband. If he doesn't change, I'm not sure I could take it (*desire*). But because I believe God commands me to be willing to live as his wife, I will choose to return and to be the best wife I can be (*goal*).
4. I would love to feel more sexual toward my husband (*desire*), but since I cannot directly control whether I feel sexual or not, I will search my heart to see if I am holding any grudge toward my husband, I will look for ways to be kind to him, and I will gradually approach him with increasing degrees of affection (*goal*).
5. With inflation, braces, and private schools, my family could really use extra money (*desire*). I will send out resumes to several companies. I will volunteer to work overtime, schedule an appointment with a financial counselor, and spend ten minutes a day in prayer concerning our finances (*goal*).
6. I would love to have an effective soul-winning ministry in our neighborhood (*desire*). Therefore I will enroll in our church's evangelism training program and will make it a point to introduce myself to at least one neighbor I do not know (*goal*).

It should be apparent that in each case the accomplishment of the *goal* increases the likelihood that the *desire* will be realized. If the man in example 5 offers to work overtime (goal), it is likely that he will add to his income (desire). There is, of course, nothing wrong with diligently working on your goals in the hope that your desires will come true, but your heart must never be set on reaching desires. The Bible instructs us to seek first God's kingdom, to lay up treasures in heaven—in other words, to set our hearts on reaching the goal of worshiping God, serving Him, and becoming more and more conformed to the image of Christ. By God's enabling grace, this goal is reachable no matter in what circumstances we find ourselves.

Paul wrote that he had learned the secret of contentment (Phil. 4:10-13). Whether his surroundings were pleasant or painful, he knew how to be content. The secret he discovered is revealed in the thirteenth verse: "I can do everything through him who gives me strength." Paul's *goal* was to please the Lord, to become increasingly like his Master. No doubt his *desires* included the freedom to preach in the churches he loved, to fellowship with his brothers and sisters, and to enjoy certain physical comforts. But whether or not his desires were met, he could always accomplish what he had set his heart on—the goal of living for God—and therefore he was content.

WHEN SHOULD WE TELL OUR PARTNERS HOW WE FEEL?

With the concept of goal and desire clearly in mind, we can properly answer the major question of this chapter: When should we express our emotions to our spouse?

Remember the principle illustrated in Ezekiel's experience: First acknowledge your emotional experience to yourself and to God, then subordinate the expression of your feelings to the purposes of God. We have seen that the biblical purpose for married people is to minister to their mates. Thus, ministry becomes the *goal*. But because we can more fully experience our value as persons when our partners minister to us, we very much want them to love and respect us. It is evident that no one can control how a mate will treat him or her. The objective of having our partners love and respect us must be regarded as a *desire*. It is something I can only pray for.

Suppose I confuse my goals and desires, as so many—perhaps most—husbands and wives tend to do. I make it my *goal* that my wife greet me warmly when I return home after a difficult day at work. If I am met at the door by a scowling woman who angrily wonders why I am late, then my goal is blocked. I feel anger. Should I share this anger with my wife? If I were to react to her hostile greeting with an expression of my irritation ("Hey, after a tough day, I wouldn't mind a smile!"), my *goal* at that moment would be to hurt her back or to stop her from complaining or to generate enough guilt to make her change. None of these motives is compatible with the goal of ministry. They are manipulative and therefore sinful.

What should I do with my anger? Consider the following actions:

Step 1: Be slow to anger. The Scriptures repeatedly exhort us to be careful when we feel angry. It is easy to express our irritation quickly for the wrong purpose and in so doing, to sin;

Step 2: Acknowledge anger. Although I am to guard against the instant, noncontrolled expression of anger, I am not to pretend the emotion is not there;

Step 3: Think through goals. I must realize that anger generally results when a goal is blocked. I should ask myself what objective I am seeking. If my partner is capable of blocking that objective, then it should never have been a goal. I need to relabel my objective as a desire ("I hope my wife greets me warmly") and to reaffirm my commitment to the goal of ministry.

Step 4: Assume responsibility for the proper goal. To put substance into my commitment, I must determine what action I can take to minister to my wife. The goal of ministry always take precedence over sharing the hurt from thwarted desires. Perhaps I could express understanding of her irritation ("Honey, I can understand that you're angry because I messed up your dinner plans") and show appreciation for her hard work ("I really appreciate the work you put into meals and laundry and everything else").

Step 5: Express negative feelings if doing so serves a good purpose. [2] I may at this point (whether two minutes or two hours later) relate to my wife my annoyance with the way I was met at the door. If I am aware of my bitter spirit, I must tell her in an effort to remove any wall of retreat created by my anger. I may also express my anger if I judge that doing so will enable her to understand better how her behavior affects me. If she wants to minister to me (as I desire), then my sharing how I feel when she behaves a certain way will help her to reach her goal of ministry better.

If I express my negative feelings after carrying out steps 1 to 4 with the purpose of keeping bitterness from taking root or of making me more understandable (and therefore more vulnerable) to my wife, then the expression of emotion can be regarded as ministry. My wife may stay angry with me for coming home late; she may consign me to an evening of hostile neglect or incessant complaint. I cannot control what she does. If she responds to me in continued anger, she is sinfully wrong and I will feel hurt and angry. But I am responsible to sustain my commitment to minister to her. My goal

---

[2]One of the most important ministries we can learn is to respond with acceptance (not necessarily agreement) when our spouses express negative feelings. At the end of this chapter is an exercise I have devised entitled "How to Respond When Your Spouse Shares Feelings" to clarify appropriate responses as I see them.

in sharing how I feel must never be to exact revenge or to change my spouse.

SUMMARY

Because our needs are met in Christ, we are free to regard marriage not as a place to fill our needs, but as a unique opportunity to help another human become more fully aware of God's love and purpose. Our goal as marriage partners must be to minister to our mates. But because we desire that our spouses minister to us, we will inevitably feel pain when they fail to respond as we wish.

Problems in communication generally involve a confusion of goals and desires. What we desire from our spouses becomes our goal. We insist that our partners treat us a certain way, and when they don't, we express our negative emotions to them either for revenge or to change them.

The essentials for establishing the kind of communication that leads to Soul Oneness are regularly reaffirming that our goal is *ministry to our spouses* and carefully ensuring that our desire for *ministry from our spouses* does not become our goal. We can express negative emotions to our spouses only after we have determined that the proper goals are in place and that our feelings arise from thwarted desires. It is never right to express to our spouses negative emotions resulting from blocked goals. A goal that my spouse can block is a wrong goal. I must set the goal of pleasing God by ministering to my spouse. With that goal firmly and functionally in place, evidenced by loving attitudes and behaviors, I am free to express the negative emotions I feel when my spouse blocks a desire.

The rest of this chapter is an exercise to develop the skill of responding to shared feelings in a way that will promote Soul Oneness.

COMMUNICATION EXERCISE:
How to Respond When Your Spouse Shares Feelings

One of the most difficult but important skills to develop as we move toward Soul Oneness through effective communication is the ability to help our spouses *feel accepted* when they share a feeling with us. Paul tells us to accept one another just as Christ also accepted us (Rom. 15:7). And Christ accepts us as we are (Rom. 5:8) and removes condemnation (Rom. 8:1), hearing and understanding and being moved by our struggles (Heb. 4:15). Therefore we can feel free to approach Him without fear as we openly express ourselves to Him (Heb. 4:16).

Nevertheless, in marriage, which is the great object lesson for the Christ-church relationship, how often we fail to accept one another as we are! How many husbands and wives have thought to themselves, "I could never tell my wife how I feel about our sex life or my fears about money or how I feel when I'm put down. Whenever I try to open up and honestly share how I feel, I just get hurt."

Many of us are not aware of the dozens of ways we convey criticism or intolerance or insensitivity when our spouses express their feelings. Whenever we respond negatively, our mates feel hurt and hide behind whatever mask protects them from further hurt—and movement toward oneness is stopped.

This exercise is designed to help you learn how to respond to your spouses' feelings in a way that will increase a sense of warmth, understanding, and closeness. I recommend that couples complete this exercise together.

There are basically two categories of response to our spouses' feelings. We can *accept* them or *reject* them. Although they are not the central part of our personality, feelings are perhaps the most delicate. When your partner tells you how he or she feels, you must treat that feeling with care, just as you would gently caress a newborn baby handed to you by its beaming mother. Too often, husbands and wives handle each others' feelings with the same care they might exercise if someone handed them a box of trash and said, "Here, get rid of this somewhere."

Read through the following interactions between a husband and wife in which one partner shares a feeling and the other responds. In each case decide whether the partner who responds (the second speaker) really communicates acceptance of the feeling. If so, circle the word *accept* that appears after the interaction. Circle *reject* if you think the response in some way constituted a rejection of the feeling. Remember that when someone really accepts your feelings, you tend to feel *understood* and *respected* and you are inclined to share warmly more of your own feelings.

Interaction 1

Wife: "I really felt hurt last night because it seemed to me that you were demanding sex from me whether I felt like it or not. I just didn't feel very important to you."

Husband: "Honey, I really didn't intend to force you into anything. I thought you wanted to make love."

Accept   *Reject*

Interaction 2

Husband: "At the Bible study last night, when I said what I thought that verse meant, you frowned and said, "Oh, I don't think it means that.' I felt like walking out and never coming back. I'm still mad about it!"

Wife: "Oh honey, I'm so sorry, I really feel badly that I did that to you."

Accept   Reject

Interaction 3

Wife: "Every time you mention my weight, I just get so frustrated that I feel like eating more, especially when you say something in front of others. I feel absolutely crushed when you say anything about my weight. I already feel bad enough about it."

Husband: "I think I sometimes say things like that just to get even for your remarks about our finances. When you tell people that we drive our old car because we can't afford a new one, I feel like it's a slam at me, and I get mad!"

Accept   Reject

Interaction 4

Husband: "Business pressures are really getting to me. I'm sick and tired of going to work. All I do is worry all day whether I'm going to make any sales. It's just too much pressure."

Wife: "Dear, maybe you should look for a job where there aren't so many pressures."

Accept   Reject

Interaction 5

Wife: "Tomorrow I have to get up and address our women's group to give a report on our project. I'm really a nervous wreck about it!"

Husband: "Honey, you'll do great! You always get nervous before something like this, but it always goes super. You don't need to be afraid."

Accept   Reject

Interaction 6

Husband: "I'm really feeling guilty about the amount of time I'm away from the family. I haven't sat down to play a game with you and the kids for months."

Wife: "I think the real problem is that you worry too much about our financial situation. That's what keeps you working so many hours. We'd all rather have less money and more of you."

Accept   Reject

Now read Interaction 1 again. A common way to reject a feeling is to *defend* or *explain* yourself after your spouse tells you how he or she feels. The effect is to tune in to how *you* feel and to miss how your spouse feels. The husband in the first interaction rejected his wife's feelings.

Look again at Interaction 2. *Apologies* offered too quickly before you let your spouse know that you understand the feelings that were shared usually mean nothing. They really amount to the message "I don't want to discuss this further and I don't really want to hear how badly I hurt you. Maybe a quick apology will end this painful conversation." *Reject* should be circled in the second interaction.

In Interaction 3, the responding husband rejected his wife's feelings with perhaps the most standard technique: *Attack.* If your spouse tells you when you made her feel bad, then informing her when she made you feel bad is a subtle but very real and devastating attack. The result will be either a long and heated series of counterattacks or a retreat into cold silence. The husband in this example clearly rejected his wife's feelings.

Consider Interaction 4. When your spouse shares a burden or struggle, don't immediately offer advice. The discouraged husband desired the encouragement of a wife who respected him, not the ideas of a counselor who thought he needed "help." Well-meaning wives often offer advice to troubled husbands, not realizing that the message their husbands hear is "Listen, you weakling, I'll tell you how to handle this, since you're making such a mess out of it!" Circle *Reject* in the fourth interaction.

Read Interaction 5 again. When your partner shares a feeling, never tell him or her not to feel "that way." Even when you are trying to be encouraging, to inform someone not to experience an emotion he or she has just expressed often comes across as a put-down. Sentences like "Honey, you shouldn't feel that way" or "There's no reason to feel so worried (hurt, etc.)" should be avoided. The responder in the fifth interaction rejected his wife's feelings.

Lastly, think through Interaction 6. Another effective but subtle technique for rejecting feelings is to correct a person's evaluation of the problem that is generating an emotion. To tell the person what the problem "really is" and what he or she should therefore be feeling does not communicate acceptance. At some point, of course, it may be necessary to suggest an accurate perception of events, but to do so immediately after a feeling is expressed conveys rejection. Once again, the sixth interaction illustrates a strategy for rejecting feelings.

I suggest that each couple reading this exercise find paper and pencils. Husbands, read the feeling shared by the wife in Interactions 1, 3, and 5. Write out a response for each one that you think would convey acceptance of the feeling. Wives, do the same for Interactions 2, 4, and 6.

After you have completed your responses, give them to your spouses. Husbands, you decide whether your wife's response would have helped you feel accepted if you had been in that situation. Wives, you evaluate whether you would feel accepted had your husband answered you with the sentence he has just written. Write the words *Accept* or *Reject* next to each other's responses depending on how you feel. Take time to talk over why you marked the responses as you did.

To complete this exercise, read the following interactions. Each one begins with a person sharing the same feeling as in the previous examples. But the responder answers with words that likely would convey acceptance of the feeling. Compare the rejecting responses in the earlier set of interactions with the accepting responses in this set.

Interaction 1

Wife: "I really felt hurt last night because it seemed that you were demanding sex from me whether I felt like it or not. I just didn't feel very important to you."

Husband: "I guess I really seemed selfish to you, as if all I cared about was what I wanted."

One good way to accept a feeling is to pretend you are a mirror *reflecting* the feeling the other person has shared.

Interaction 2

Husband: "At the Bible study last week, when I said what I thought that verse meant, you frowned and said, 'Oh I don't think it means that.' I felt like walking out and never coming back. I'm still mad about it!"

Wife: "I'm not sure I understand what made you feel so angry. Did you feel that I was putting you down?"

Listen carefully to what your spouse is saying. If you're not sure you really understand what is being expressed, *explore* what was meant by asking questions. Your partner will likely interpret this to mean that you really want to know what he or she felt.

Interaction 3

Wife: "Everytime you mention my weight, I just get so frustrated that I feel like eating more, especially when you say something in front of others. I feel absolutely crushed when you say something about my weight. I already feel bad enough about it."

Husband: "Honey, it sounds to me that you really feel hurt that I don't seem to accept and love you as you are. Is that right?"

Another way to accept a feeling is to *clarify* what your spouse has shared. Describe the way you think he or she is feeling and ask if you heard correctly.

Interaction 4

Husband: "Business pressures are really getting to me. I'm sick and tired of going to work. All I do is worry all day whether I'm going to make any sales. It's just too much pressure."

Wife: "Honey, the pressures must really be difficult. I remember that you once told me that this isn't the job you really wanted. I wonder if some of the problem isn't frustration over being stuck in this line of work.

A fourth way to accept feelings is to *extend* what you've heard, not denying what was said, but suggesting other feelings that may be related to what was shared.

Interaction 5

Wife: "Tomorrow I have to get up and address our women's group to give a report on our project. I'm really a nervous wreck about it!"

I suggest that all you *wives* reading this book write a response that makes you feel accepted.

Interaction 6

Husband: "I'm really feeling guilty about the amount of time I'm away from the family. I haven't played a game with you and the kids for months."

Let me request now that all you *husbands* write a response that would help you feel accepted.

The following chart summarizes the major points in this exercise:

HOW TO RESPOND WHEN YOUR SPOUSE SHARES FEELINGS: SOME GUIDELINES

Ways to Reject Feelings

1. *Defend/explain*

   "The reason I said that . . ."
   "What I meant was . . ."

2. *Apologize*

   "I'm really sorry that . . ."
   "I shouldn't have said that . . ."

3. *Attack*

   "I admit what I did was wrong, but you . . ."
   "Well, maybe you're right, but what I can't understand is why you . . ."

4. *Advise*

   "Maybe you should . . ."
   "It seems to me that if you . . ."

5. *Disdain*

   "I don't really see why you feel . . ."
   "Gee, honey, there's no need to feel . . ."

6. Correct

"What I think you really mean is . . ."
"I don't think you feel . . ."

Ways to Accept Feelings

1. Reflect

"It sounds as if you feel . . ."
"Guess you really felt . . . when . . ."

2. Clarify

"Are you saying that `. . .?"
"I wonder if you feel . . ."

3. Explore

"I'm not sure what you mean . . ."
"When else do you feel like that? I don't quite understand how you feel about . . ."

4. Extend

"You really felt. . . . Did you also feel . . .?"
"I can see that you feel. . . . If I were in your shoes, I might also feel. . . . Do you feel like that?"

5

BODY ONENESS:
Physical Pleasure
With Personal Meaning

If poor communication heads the list of marital complaints, sexual problems run a close second. Nowhere does disharmony between spouses express itself more painfully than in the bedroom.

Here is a sampling of the concerns I hear regularly in my counseling:

"I feel so used by my husband. When he wants sex, he expects me to be ready at a moment's notice. And he never will stop at just hugging me. We always end up in the bedroom. It's made me pull away from him physically."

"I can't understand why my wife is so unresponsive. I'd settle for a warm kiss once in a while, but at best all I get is mechanical cooperation. It sure makes it hard not to look somewhere else for satisfaction. I can't understand why she isn't more willing to meet my sexual needs."

"I've never had an orgasm, I don't think. And I feel terrible about it! I guess I feel cheated when I see how much my husband enjoys his climax. And to make it worse, I can't tell him the truth—I fake an orgasm. He'd be really upset if he knew he doesn't satisfy me."

"My wife just isn't attractive to me anymore. She's critical, bossy, and overweight. She would never dress in the kind of sexy clothes I like. Now I couldn't care less what she wears. I'm just not interested anymore in putting together a good sex life with her."

"Do you think oral sex is wrong? My husband and I get along really well, except for this. He really wants me to do it, but just the idea turns me off. He says that if I really loved him, I'd be willing to at least give it a try."

"Everything in our marriage is basically O.K. but our sex life just isn't right. Neither of us has any special problems with it, but we always wait till we're exhausted, and then it's more like a duty. There's just no romance to it."

Imagine yourself in the role of the counselor. What would you do to help these people? What are the problems behind their sexual difficulties: poor technique, insecurity, psychological hang-ups, selfishness, different levels of sex drive? Exactly what *should* a Christian couple experience in the privacy of their bedroom?

So far in this book, I have suggested that an intimate relationship between husband and wife is nourished by the growth of *Spirit Oneness,* a turning to the Lord rather than to one's spouse to find security and significance, and *Soul Oneness,* a commitment to minister to the spouse's needs rather than manipulating to meet one's own needs.

The goal of oneness in marriage involves a third element. This element is too often regarded as central to a relationship, but it is happily necessary to complete the biblical picture of marital oneness. A human being is not only a *Spirit* capable of relating personally to God, and a *Soul* able to relate personally to other people, but also a *Body,* a physical being equipped with five senses for relating as a body to other bodies. We can *touch* each other's bodies, *smell* them, often *see* and *hear* the noises they make, and even *taste* them. People can interact with their bodies.

Just as God has graciously provided instructions for our personal relationships, so has He also communicated a special design for our physical relationships. Following this design will result in a pleasurable and meaningful sexual relationship between husband and wife. In this chapter I will first explain what Body Oneness is and then tell how it can be developed.

BODY ONENESS VS. FUN SEX

Married couples who seek counseling because of sexual difficulties often ask for less than what God wants to provide. Too often a man will want no more than to learn ejaculatory control and a woman will express a desire for more frequent orgasms. Perhaps the most typical request is for help in reducing tensions in the bedroom and in somehow finding a way for both partners to warmly anticipate and enjoy the sexual experience.

As I read the romantic story in the Song of Solomon and meditate on the intended richness of the marriage union—so rich that it serves as a living parable of the bond between Christ and His bride—I cannot help but think that Christian couples are short-changing themselves when all they want from their sexual relationship is more pleasure and less frustration. I am not suggesting that we pursue some sort of "spiritualized sex" untouched by sheer sensual pleasure, but I do believe our sexual make-up equips us to enjoy much more than a really good climax. To splash about in a puddle when God provides an ocean is no noble self-denial. It is worse than foolish. It not only robs us of intended blessing, but robs God of glory and the joy of giving.

Let me clarify this by making a distinction between Body Oneness and what I call "Fun Sex." As is his custom, Satan has counterfeited what God offers to committed Christians. It is quite clear—and the testimony of thousands affirms—that the only requirement for sexual pleasure is the proper positioning of two cooperative bodies. No emotional relationship between the two persons is needed. A man once told me that while he was in the service, he had sexual relations with dozens of women and never knew even one of them by name. Yet the sex itself was physically pleasurable to him. When I refer to sheer physical pleasure as Fun Sex, I am simply contrasting it with Frustrating, Dull, Tension-filled Sex. In no way do I suggest that only sinful sex can be fun.

Body Oneness is different from Fun Sex—and better. I use the term to refer to a physical relationship that a Christian couple can enjoy who know something of the reality of Spirit and Soul Oneness. The distinction can be stated simply: Fun Sex involves physical pleasure without legitimate personal meaning. Body Oneness involves physical pleasure with personal meaning. Let me develop these concepts.

Fun Sex

Something has gone wrong with the sexual drive. The natural appetite for erotic pleasure has become a mad tyrant, demanding fulfillment with no concern for either boundaries or consequences. Ruined reputations, shattered relationships, prematurely ended ministries—no price seems too high to pay for the pleasures of sex. Why? Why has the biological desire for sexual fun become a slavemaster, driving people to disregard God's standards?

One of the great errors of our day is the growing tendency to think of people as nothing more then intricate and self-conscious organizations of physical matter, collections of chemicals that come together during gestation and disintegrate after death. Words like *soul* and *spirit* are largely devoid of any substantive meaning and serve only as inspiring rhetoric to elegantly describe how the human machine functions. Nothing exists but matter—bones, organs, skin, and hair.

Something called the "human potential movement" has

rightly rebelled against such dehumanizing theory, insisting that people are more than mortal bodies. We are persons, say the humanists, real persons whose worth and value cannot be reduced to our material nature.

For many of us, the affirmation that we are more than machines has a certain appeal. A large segment of our society may be willing to regard a fetus as merely a bit of tissue, but somehow we rebel at the suggestion that the cooing infant in our arms is simply an emotional, squirming machine. Clearly, we want to think of people—at least the ones we like or value—as persons and not as machines.

But there is a problem. If we refuse—as most humanists do—to believe that life began with a personal Creator, then all talk of people as more than impersonal, complex machines amounts to nothing more than satisfying delusion. For something impersonal to give birth to something personal is as reasonable as expecting a rock to evolve into a dog. To speak of the value of persons without a living, personal God as the ultimate beginning is folly.

With God out of the picture, there is neither basis for regarding ourselves as truly personal (more than bodies) nor resources to satisfy personal needs. If we are nothing more than physical machines, then we really have no personal needs.

Now, what if we are just bodies? About the best we can do with a body is to provide it with subjectively pleasurable sensations. "Creature comforts" we call them: food that tastes good, wine that generates merry feelings, mattresses that are comfortable, fancy cars that give us pride and satisfaction as we pick up our friends, country clubs that offer doormen, maître-d's, and caddies who relieve us of the burden of opening our own doors, selecting our own tables, or lugging our own golf clubs. The goal is to make our bodies comfortable and filled with pleasant feelings.

The real tragedy of denying our character as persons made in the image of a personal God is that very few people are aware of the exhilarating potential for *personal* satisfaction. We have missed the truth that the deepest joys and satisfactions do not come through the five senses. Even Christians who really should know better try to relieve *personal* pain with *physical* pleasure. When we hurt from rejection, emptiness, fear, or loneliness, the temptation to gain relief by pleasantly arousing our physical senses is almost irresistible. We snack on potato chips when we're bored, climb into a hot tub when we're tense, masturbate when we feel alone—something, anything to replace the ache in our hearts with good feelings.

No bodily sensation is quite so intensely pleasurable or all-consuming as sexual arousal and release. If we regard ourselves merely as bodies and if we therefore want more than anything else to find some way to feel physically good, then sex is the ticket. And the pursuit of sexual pleasure can become a strong preoccupation. The compulsive craving for erotic excitement prevalent in our society is rooted in our denial of ourselves as real persons made for personal fellowship with God and others.

Women who wrestle with personal insecurities (e.g., "My husband doesn't seem to really care about me") often turn to food, new clothes, or fulfilling jobs to numb the pain of feeling unloved. But there is no better anesthetic for personal pain than sexual intimacy. The bodily pleasure of sexual release convincingly counterfeits—at least for the moment—the personal joy of true security.

Men who are tormented with doubts about personal adequacy that rob them of peace and self-respect can quickly find a hassle-free substitute for masculine fulfillment through sex. Scores of men handle their wives' rejection by having an affair or purchasing a pornographic magazine or masturbating while watching an X-rated movie in their fantasy. And it works: for a short time they feel really good.

But—rather than relieving or resolving the personal problems that result from rejection or criticism, sexual pleasure merely camouflages the pain with physical sensations. The situation is like a man with a brain tumor getting drunk: although he feels no pain, he is still dying.

The unresolved personal disorder—a lack of security and significance—still clamors for attention. And the demand is often felt as a strong urge to experience even more physical pleasure. A vicious circle is set into motion: the anesthesia of sexual pleasure for personal pain drives the pain out of awareness where it is experienced no longer as a *personal* problem but as an urge for more *physical* pleasure; more pleasure then renders the pain less recognizable as personal and increases its felt demand for physical relief, which leads to further sexual experiences—and on to the point of absolute degeneracy. What begins as an effort to relieve a problem ends not in real solutions but additional problems. Guilt, rationalization, further enslavement to inner urges, unanswered personal questions—the wages of sin is death. The way seems right, but the end is personal destruction.

Few affairs (including homosexual ones) are motivated simply by desire for the physical pleasure of the sexual orgasm. Although that unique thrill is a strong temptation in itself, the *compulsive appeal* of sex so evident in our society's frantic search for more pleasure grows out of the opportunity that sex affords to feel a welcome and exciting relief from the steady, throbbing pain of insecurity and insignificance.

My major point is this: Sex provides a *physical* solution for a *personal* problem. The evil thing is that it seems to work so well. During those few magic moments of sexual climax, a person experiences a consuming excitement in the body that counterfeits a sense of wholeness in the soul. Satan's most convincing imitation of the enduring and real *personal* worth available in Christ is the temporary but intense *bodily* pleasure of sex. He seeks to persuade us that when our bodies are tingling with sexual excitement, we have reached the ultimate in our potential for satisfaction—there is nothing deeper to be enjoyed. And his argument is convincing to the degree that we regard ourselves as mere bodies evolved from impersonal matter and not as real persons made in the image of a personal God.

So Satan does offer Fun Sex: sex that for a moment helps a woman feel desirable, feminine, wanted, secure; sex that enables a man to feel attractive, adequate, manly, significant. But Satan cannot offer meaningful relationship built on loving commitment to one another. Fun Sex is a charade. It satisfies the body but leaves the real person empty and despairing. It offers pleasure for the body without meaning for the person.

Body Oneness

God offers something more than Fun Sex. His design for Body Oneness provides us not only with the legitimate physical pleasure of sexual intimacy, but also with meaning. Body Oneness includes pleasure for the body *and* rich meaning for the person. Consider how this works.

Personal meaning in God's world depends finally on participation in God's purposes. To build something that has no eternal impact but will disappear like castles in the sand is *not* meaningful. But to have a part in erecting a structure that will never crumble *is* meaningful. The marriage relationship is one of God's creations for building up people. It gives husbands and wives the chance to minister to an immortal human being in a uniquely intimate fashion. To enjoy the meaningfulness of marriage, then, requires a once-made but ongoing commitment of mutual ministry to build up our mates. The more we see opportunities to minister to our mates and the more we seize them, the more meaning our marriage will have. This is the Soul Oneness we examined earlier.

But while I am trying to minister to my wife's personal needs, I sense needs within me. It is at this point I must take very seriously the conviction that nearness to God is my only good, that He alone is sufficient to satisfy what I need to live as I should. Upon reckoning what is true—that I am secure and significant in Christ—I must by faith approach my wife as a personally full husband, willing to share the love shed abroad in my heart, needing nothing in return. When she reacts with loving respect, I feel great. When she reacts with something else like neglect or criticism or indifference, I will hurt—but I must hold firmly onto the truth that I am whole in Christ and therefore not threatened by my wife's response. The more that spouses react to each other on the basis of their perceived fullness in Christ, the more their marriage will progress toward Spirit Oneness.

A personally meaningful marriage depends on the development of Soul Oneness. And Soul Oneness cannot grow without Spirit Oneness. When both levels of oneness are present, the relationship is vital and intimate. Core parts of the personality are touched and engaged. Communication reaches beneath the routineness of "What's for supper?" or "Where shall we go on vacation?" or "Do you want to have sex? It's been a month." An awareness of unusual closeness develops, not in a steady rhythm, but in erratic outbursts that gradually diminish in intensity and increase in frequency toward a pattern of generally increasing unity. Then a couple, in their sexual activity, enjoy each other's body in the rich *personal* union that already exists. The phrase "make love" fits poorly. "Expressing love" is better. The Song of Songs celebrates the intoxicating pleasure of sexual activity between two persons who are united by loving commitment. The two *bodies* that come together house two *persons* who are already together.

The Book of Proverbs instructs young men to avoid sexual pleasure with any available woman but to fully enjoy body contact with one's wife. By itself, sexual excitement is one thing; the physical union of two persons deeply in love with each other in a relationship of Spirit and Soul Oneness is quite another.

I have defined Body Oneness as pleasure for the body and meaning for the person. Let me now offer a more complete description. Body Oneness is—

- Sexual pleasure between a couple who depend on the Lord to meet their needs and are committed to being used of God in meeting each other's needs;
- Sexual pleasure that grows out of a commitment to minister to one's spouse in the physical realm by giving maximum sexual pleasure;
- Sexual pleasure that provides a shared experience of sensual excitement and sexual satisfaction;
- Sexual pleasure that heightens each partner's awareness of their unbreakable bond.

OVERCOMING OBSTACLES TO BODY ONENESS

If God intends that husbands and wives enjoy sex, why is it so often a source of argument, boredom, and disappointment rather than harmony, excitement, and fulfillment? If the philanderers of this world are to be believed, the Fun Sex available in the motel is far more enjoyable than the feeble attempts at Body Oneness in the marital bedroom. One husband told me that he was impotent with his Christian wife and erotically alive with his pagan girlfriend. To him, biblical morality was an invitation to a celibate life.

If the choice is between Fun Sex or Body Oneness, most people—Christian or not—would likely opt for sexual pleasure *with* personal meaning. But for many, the alternatives seem to be Fun Sex (pleasure without meaning) or No Oneness (neither pleasure nor meaning). Small wonder that professing Christians in increasing numbers are stepping across the line of morality, leaving behind a bad relationship and sexual frustration in search of something that at least feels good.

Our society needs no reminder that sexual pleasure is available. People do not need a biblical relationship of marital oneness (or any sort of personal relationship) to enjoy Fun Sex. It is also clear—and discouraging to many Christian couples—that efforts to develop a personal relationship often seem to interfere with rather than to enhance sexual pleasure. When a couple engage in the hard work of opening up to each other while striving to work out their commitment to ministry, they open the door to conflicts, unhealed wounds, and unresolved tensions that sometimes act like water on sexual sparks.

Why should this be? God's design prohibits sex except in marriage. But the very effort to carry out the marriage vows by developing a close relationship gets in the way of sexual pleasure. Yet God wants us to experience the joys of sex within a growing personal relationship. The rest of this chapter explains why marriage can be the worst environment for experiencing sexual pleasure, but how we can make it the perfect environment for achieving Body Oneness.

In recent years, beginning with Masters and Johnson's controversial but enlightening research, much attention has been focused on human sexual responsiveness.[1] Emerging from this extensive research is the understanding that three overlapping kinds of problems have the potential to decrease sexual interest and interfere with the normal sexual pattern of arousal and orgasmic release. These problems are—

1. *Problems in the Person:* Personal hang-ups or psychological inhibitions often traceable to past experiences of emotional pain that somehow involved sexuality (e.g., rape, incest, punishment for sexual curiosity);

2. *Problems Between the Partners:* Relational tensions stemming from communication problems, irritation and resentment, fear of rejection, guilt for past indiscretions, etc.;

3. *Problems With Technique:* Inadequate knowledge of how to relate sexually to a partner in a way that promotes desire, arousal, and climax.

Of all these, the problems with technique are most readily corrected. The other two kinds of problems involve more stubborn personal difficulties and require greater insight and painful emotional work to overcome. This is undoubtedly one reason why some people elect to travel the wide, smooth, short path to Fun Sex rather than the narrow, bumpy, longer road to Body Oneness.

Christians, of course, are not allowed this option. We are commanded to do the hard work of building a relationship as a foundation for our enjoyment of sex. Fun Sex is less than God intends for us; He never endorses a counterfeit. And He supplies the resources for us to walk the narrow road that leads to Body Oneness. But what are these resources? Let's look at the means Christ provides for overcoming these three obstacles to Body Oneness.

Problems in the Person

To my mind, all the problems that we label "emotional hangups" or "psychological disorders" are the symptoms of unmet personal needs. People who are afraid to trust anyone, to be open, to

[1]William H. Masters and Virginia E. Johnson, *Human Sexual Responses* (Boston: Little, Brown & Co., 1966).

make decisions, or to relax rather than work have never understood deeply enough the security and significance available in Jesus Christ. Beneath the *appearance* of psychological problems is the *reality* of unmet needs for personal worth. These needs remain unmet because people find it difficult to take God at His word and act on the fact that in Christ they are both secure and significant. Consider an example.

A little girl is molested by her father. This confusing, painful experience may teach her that men are a source of hurt and must never be trusted. Perhaps she grows up believing that her security needs cannot be met and that it would be wise to protect herself from rejection by keeping some sort of distance between herself and men.

One day she marries. Her husband is looking forward to their first night together. When he approaches her, something happens: she freezes inside, she feels nervous, tight. Her husband struggles to be patient but cannot conceal his disappointment and frustration. She feels terrible. She wonders what is wrong with her. Time doesn't help. As the months pass, she withdraws from sexual involvement more and more, eager to avoid the emotional pain. Her husband tries a few lackluster seductions, then quits, and settles into a pattern of mechanical release whenever her guilt prompts her to "service" him. When this couple sit together in church, there is no warmth between them; a jointly held hymnbook is the extent of their oneness. Fulfilling, pleasurable sex seems like the impossible dream. The beginning of the tragedy is a Problem in the Person, in this case, the wife.

Notice the core of her problem. She is controlled by *fear* based on the *wrong belief* that if she gives herself to her husband, and if he in any way mistreats her, she would then be face to face with the pain of insecurity. Her problem must not be defined as the childhood molesting. Certainly that was terrible, but the real damage lay in its effect on what she *believes*. For years her life has been governed by the assumption that sexual closeness with a man contains a legitimate threat to her security as a woman.

But the assumption is simply not true. For the Christian, the basic need to be loved and to feel secure in a relationship is fully met in Christ. Yet this woman has not acted on the basis of that truth. She is still depending on her husband to provide her with security, but because of her belief that closeness means more insecurity, she has backed away from him, making Body Oneness impossible.

The solution here is *not* to gain greater confidence that her husband will not hurt her, but to challenge her belief that sexual closeness poses a valid threat to her need for love. If her need for love is truly met by the God of love, then rejection from her husband may be legitimately *painful* but not *threatening.* Her need for security remains fully met because of Christ's unchanging faithfulness.

On the strength of this correct belief, she must jump from her Cliff of Safety—to use the metaphor of chapter 2—into the Chasm of Whatever She Fears the Most, trusting only in the Lord's love to preserve her. In counseling, I would then ask her to *decide* that she will not avoid anything because of a fear of rejection. The next step would be to set up a program of deliberately choosing to do what she fears—the practical side of cliff-jumping. Perhaps she will need to reestablish some sort of relationship with her dad. Certainly she must approach her husband for sex: a homework assignment might be to snuggle up to him on the couch during a TV show rather than busying herself in the kitchen.

One woman I counseled agreed to put her hand on her husband's thigh as they watched TV. She was to repeat to herself, "Lord, right now I'm terrified he might reach over and want to do more. But I believe that I am a loved, secure woman because of you, so I'll minister to my husband no matter what he wants or how afraid I feel."

At the next session she reported that the truth of God's love seemed to bore a hole deep into her brain as she chose to jump from her cliff of safe withdrawal into the abyss of feeling used and dirty. The rope of Christ's love held. Rather than being destroyed, she became whole. She did not feel used, but useful.

Thus, Problems in the Person can be thought of as evidence of unmet personal needs, which remain unmet because of (1) a refusal to believe that in Christ we are already secure and significant, and (2) a fear-motivated unwillingness to act on this belief by doing whatever scares us the most.

It should be clear that in conceptual terms, the solution to Problems in the Person that interfere with Body Oneness is to develop Spirit Oneness—trust in Christ to meet our personal needs, evidenced by a willingness to do whatever is right in spite of tremendous fear.

Problems Between the Partners

A second category of obstacles to Body Oneness involves problems of relationship between the persons. Even though the tensions between partners have their beginning in the individuals themselves, a whole set of problems needs to be remedied by them together.

When people do not depend fully on the Lord to satisfy their essential needs, they necessarily turn to others. Their purpose becomes to arrange their worlds of people and things in a way that brings some sense of satisfaction. The goal of manipulation—attempting to change whatever does not satisfy so that it will satisfy—is set in motion. Husbands try to make their wives lose weight, stop nagging, be more cooperative sexually, and acquiesce to their opinions. Wives work hard to get their husbands to play less golf, help more with housework, be more romantic, spend more time with the children, and share feelings more openly.

One key difficulty with these manipulative goals (which seem so reasonable—"After all, shouldn't he spend more time at home?") is that they all violate a cardinal rule of mental heath: *Never assume responsibility for a goal you cannot control.* No person can ever fully control the response of another. Influence yes, control no.

Suppose your spouse refuses to be manipulated. You cannot guarantee that your efforts to change the other will be effective. Perhaps, as often happens, pressure to change results in change—but change in a direction opposite to what is desired. What then?

When a goal is not reached, people experience either anxiety, resentment, or guilt. If a husband's goal is to gain his wife's respect for a certain decision he has made, and if she responds with bewildered disagreement ("You did *what?*"), he will likely feel angry and *resentful.* His wife has blocked his goal.

Suppose a wife's goal is to be treated gently and kindly. In the past, her husband has been known to make cutting comments about her in front of others. In a group, she is nervous about what he might say. Because her manipulative goal is precarious, she will feel *anxious.*

Consider a man raised by perfectionistic parents. He may set the goal of never disappointing his wife and children, believing that only by setting a consistent example of spiritual maturity can he regard himself as worthwhile. Whenever he thinks he has let his family down ("I know you're tired, dad, so we can play ball tomorrow"), this burdened man will feel *guilt.* Although his goal is unreachable, he will likely berate himself for failing to reach it.[2]

These three troublesome emotions all tend to inhibit sexual

---

[2]See *Effective Biblical Counseling* for a more complete discussion of how wrong goals lead to resentment, anxiety, and guilt.

arousal. It is difficult to feel angry with your spouse and sensual at the same time. If you are nervous around your partner, you will have trouble getting into the relaxed frame of mind vital to sexual interest. Similarly, a weight of guilt will block sexual excitement.

It is fair to say that problems between partners that inhibit enjoyable sex can be traced to manipulative goals. Communication difficulties, lack of time together, and failure to share openly can all be understood as the result of self-centered goals. The accompanying resentment, anxiety, and guilt that block the growth of Body Oneness are a part of this evil package of mutual manipulation.

It obviously will do no good to instruct an angry husband, a worried wife, or a guilt-ridden partner to feel different. The remedy is to change goals. Shift from manipulating your spouse to meet your needs to ministering to your spouse's needs. When this shift takes place, these debilitating emotions slowly give way to compassion and warmth. Why?

1. The goal of ministering cannot be blocked by your spouse. There is therefore no trigger for *resentment* toward your partner;

2. Fulfilling the goal of ministry depends only on your willingness. The *anxiety* of wondering what your mate will do is eliminated.

3. The goal of representing the Lord to your spouse is reachable, at least as a basic direction. Although everyone occasionally fails, the resources of confession, forgiveness, repentance, and enabling are available to get back on the track and grow in consistency. There is no warrant for self-preoccupying *guilt.*

To remove problems to Body Oneness, people need to examine their moment-by-moment goals as they interact with their mates, confess wrong goals of manipulation, and set right goals of ministry. And that is what it takes to develop Soul Oneness. Obviously, Body Oneness can only exist as an outgrowth of Spirit and Soul Oneness. If you are having sexual problems, first examine how you are failing to develop Spirit and Soul Oneness.

Problems With Technique

Some couples are trusting God to meet their personal needs and are committed to mutual ministry, but still do not have a good sexual relationship. Sometimes the problem involves an insufficient or incorrect knowledge of the art of lovemaking.

In certain circles, one almost gets the impression that to know of the intricacies of sexual functioning and to be a romantic, skilled sexual partner is somehow less than spiritual. But ignorance of how to sexually arouse and satisfy one's spouse brings no glory to the One who created sex in the first place.

It is surprising how many men simply do not know what arouses and satisfies a woman. They lack awareness that the clitoris and not the vagina is her primary organ of sexual sensitivity, lack understanding of her need for warm and tender caresses, and lack appreciation for her desire for a romantic prelude rather than the "let's-go-do-it" approach.

On the other hand, many women fail to recognize the impact of visual stimuli such as provocative clothing. They do not understand the threat implied in their bored consent, mechanical servicing, or irritated turndowns. They may be ignorant of technical matters such as how to help a man delay his ejaculation.

I recommend *The Act of Marriage* by Tim and Beverly LaHaye and *Intended for Pleasure* by Ed and Gaye Wheat as two excellent books that explain how our sexual natures work. Both volumes offer an explicit but tasteful discussion of the details of human sexuality presented within a clearly biblical framework.[3]

Secular works such as those by Masters and Johnson and Helen Singer Kaplan, though written with no concern for biblical values, present useful descriptions of sexual physiology, love-making techniques, and corrective measures for various sexual problems. When read carefully by mature Christians capable of discerning proper and improper values, these books can offer real help.[4]

Body Oneness, the experience of sexual pleasure that expresses the personal oneness of spirit and soul, is part of God's plan for total marital oneness. A marriage that is developing all three aspects of oneness—Spirit, Soul, and Body—provides a couple with a living parable of the eternal union of Christ and His bride, the church.

The goal of marriage, then, is—

• Spirit Oneness: Trusting in Christ alone to meet your personal needs for security and significance;

• Soul Oneness: Ministering to your partner in a way that enhances an awareness of his or her worth in Christ;

• Body Oneness: Enjoying sexual pleasure as an expression and outgrowth of a personal relationship.

---

[3] *The Act of Marriage* (Grand Rapids: Zondervan, 1976); *Intended for Pleasure* (Old Tappan, N.J.: Fleming H. Revell, 1977, rev. 1981).

[4] Among works by William H. Masters and Virginia E. Johnson are *Human Sexual Response* (Boston: Little, Brown & Co., 1966), and *Human Sexual Inadequacy* (New York: Bantam, 1980); by Helen Singer Kaplan are *The New Sex Therapy: Active Treatment of Sexual Dysfunctions* (New York: Times Books, 1974); *Making Sense of Sex* (New York: Simon & Schuster, 1979); and *The Disorder of Sexual Desire* (New York: Simon & Schuster, 1979).

Part II
BUILDING
THE FOUNDATION

Introduction

Christianity is poorly advertised by "Christian Marriages" that are no better than marital relationships governed by secular values and empowered by merely human energy. If we are to display the love and power of Christ effectively in our marriages, we must first realize that nothing less is expected of us than consistent movement toward Total Oneness: Oneness in Spirit, Oneness in Soul, Oneness in Body.

A Christian couple have the resources to develop a depth of intimacy that far surpasses a successful marriage between unbelievers. Yet too many Christians never advance beyond mutual toleration or comfortable compatibility. To understand God's design for marriage, I have presented in part I my understanding of what a biblical marriage should be.

If we think of part I as an architect's blueprint, then perhaps we can visualize the completed structure of such a marriage. The substantial problem that remains is to transform the artist's sketch into a living, experienced reality. For some, the problem is greater than for others; for no one is the problem insurmountable.

The first step is to turn the blueprint over to the building contractor. When he studies the plans, he must determine precisely what materials are needed to complete the structure. This is my concern in part II. I attempt to describe the building blocks we must bring to the construction site of our marriage if we intend to build a relationship of Total Oneness.

I have asked many people in my counseling office to define the essentials for a happy marriage, and the variety of the responses has been as numerous as the respondents. In my judgment, a tragically high number of marriages fail to achieve real oneness, not because the spouses weren't trying hard, but because they were not working with the right materials. The carpenter may swing a hammer with force and accuracy, but without good wood and nails, the effort is wasted. No matter what else may be right about a relationship—sincerity, honest effort, noble aspirations, warm feelings, common beliefs, communication skills—a marriage will not and cannot reach the goal of oneness without the basics.[1]

What are these essentials, the building blocks of marriage? Are they readily available? How long must we wait for them to arrive once we place our order? Are they priced beyond the reach of all but the spiritually wealthy? Do they come with "directions for assembly" that only a professional marriage builder can understand?

If I read the Bible correctly, the good news is that the required building blocks are few in number, available on demand, in plentiful supply, free for the taking, and accompanied by instructions that are simple enough that only sincere motivation is required to understand them and yet profound enough to offer an unending challenge to the mature believer.

The building blocks required for the development of oneness in marriage are—

1. Grace
2. Commitment
3. Acceptance

The order is significant. We cannot have real commitment without first having grace. And it is impossible to accept our spouses as we need to accept them without first being committed to them. Let us arrange the elements in hierarchical order.

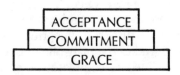

The next three chapters explain what constitutes each of these building blocks.

---

[1] If your goal is subbiblical (e.g., to achieve a level of compatibility that leads to mutual enjoyment), it is possible to fulfill it without these building blocks. I am writing this book for those who want all that God provides and have set the proper goal.

6
Building Block 1: GRACE

A deacon sat across from me and shook his head in anger and desperation.

"I've taught Sunday School for twenty years. I have even taught courses on the Christian home. You can't tell me much about the Bible that I don't already know. And I have tried—God knows I've tried—to the best of my ability to be the husband, father, deacon, and businessman God wants me to be. Things have gone well, real well, in the church and in my business. But no matter what I do, I can't get my marriage together.

"Right now, I'm so frustrated, angry, and miserable that I'm ready to quit. And I met somebody else. Look, I know it's wrong, so don't give me a lecture on sin—but if you knew the frustrations I live with at home, maybe you'd understand how much I need to just talk and relax with a woman. We haven't slept together, but God knows I want to. She's just so different from my wife. I cannot get it together with my wife—and I've tried hard for a long time. We've been married twenty-two years, and I never so much as looked at another woman until now. I want to please the Lord, I really do, but there's just no way to make my marriage work."

If you were the counselor, what would you say? If I were to present my thoughts on oneness in marriage, I would likely meet with a wan smile, a disgusted shaking of the head, and finally a comment such as "Sounds good. Hope it works for you. But it can't work in my marriage. I've tried!" Lectures on working toward the goal of becoming a biblical husband whether his wife changes or not would probably suffer a similar fate. To point out that a good marriage must be regarded as a legitimate desire for which to pray, but that becoming a good husband is a goal for which he must assume responsibility would stand little chance of replacing his despair with an eager spirit of cooperation.

What is the problem? What is lacking in this man's attitude that blocks any hope of progress? We need to look beneath the man's sinful behavior and see that he refuses to *believe* certain basic truths. Rebellious unbelief is the core of sin; rebellious actions are its visible expression.

Effective resolution of this man's problem requires first that we identify the central questions he is answering incorrectly. As I see it, this despairing husband is controlled by a wrong answer to a good question: "Is there sufficient reason why I should not regard this marriage as a catastrophe that justifies my despair? Is there any reason to expend further efforts to respond biblically?"

The question is legitimate. Yet it is tempting to skirt the tough questions or to provide stock answers that deserve no more than token assent. To tell this husband to love his wife as he should because Christ is sufficient for his needs and because the Bible tells him to do so is good advice that will not be heard. There is no point in saying it. Before this man will work on his marriage, he must have reason to believe that it makes sense to do so.

I recall a godly woman relating her frustration that her unsaved husband had shown no interest in sex for years. She was feeling not only personal rejection, but sexual frustration. Prayer and Bible reading had given her strength to carry on without sinfully handling her frustration, but renewed efforts to be warmly accepting and sensually appealing had failed to stir her husband at all sexually. With some embarrassment she asked, "What am I to do with my sexual desire? Sometimes my body seems to literally scream for fulfillment."

Beneath this woman's legitimate problem of sexual frustration there lies a deeper concern: "This situation seems utterly intolerable. I'm not asking whether I should masturbate or have an affair. What I'm really wondering is whether this problem warrants despair. If so, then I will compromise my standards to obtain relief. If not, then I am willing to remain moral." This concern must be addressed before exhortations to live biblically will be heard meaningfully.

Another woman nervously told me that her father, a highly esteemed pastor, had molested her repeatedly during her preteen and early teenage years. She sought counseling to thaw out a frozen response to her husband's sexual advances. "I'm not sure if I can ever really give myself to my husband sexually. I know I should. I want to be one in spirit, soul, and body and I heard what you said about jumping off cliffs and making ourselves do what seems impossible. But I've tried! And my husband has been wonderfully patient. But nothing helps. It's been six years! I don't see how I can ever feel good about sex. The effects of my dad's sin are just too deep."

Reminders that God's love is sufficient for her needs and further encouragement to approach her husband sexually miss the point. Her real question is not "What should I do?" but rather "Is there any hope?"

These are tough questions from a despairing husband, a frustrated wife, and a victim of another's sin. The struggle will not be calmed with responses like "Things will get better" or "If you try harder, God will bless" or "Stop feeling sorry for yourself and live as you should." The deeper question remains: "Is there any point to obedience, or is despair justified?"

I suppose there has never been a marriage between two honest, self-examining people that at some time has not reached a seemingly irredeemable low point. There have been moments in my own marriage when the wall between my wife and me seemed too high to hurdle, too thick to break. We found it hard to muster hope. It was not easy to be confident that somehow the barriers blocking our oneness could be removed.

What should a couple do when they are faced with these desperate questions? A student who is concerned that he or she cannot pass the exam will not be motivated by a seminar on study techniques. We cannot cultivate interest in following biblical direction if we believe nothing good can happen. Before the responsibilities of marriage will be regarded as inviting opportunities rather than pointless duties, the core of a person's attitude must shift from despair to hope. To effect this shift requires that we provide adequate answers to the tough questions.

In a world where *every* relationship is gnarled by the deforming effects of sin, nothing is needed more than an appreciation of the grace of God as a foundation for hope. To be fully persuaded that there is always reason to live responsibly no matter what may go wrong is indispensable to the Christian life. Too many unhappy spouses, however, claim promises that God never made as their foundation of hope. They trust that if they do all they can, God will change their spouses into the loving Christians they should be. But a reason to live *never* consists of a guarantee that "Things will get better" or that "God will save your husband and help him stop drinking." The hope of the Christian is far deeper than a mere change in someone else. The hope of the Christian is inescapably bound up in the grace of God.

It would be easy to quote a few verses from Hebrews (especially 6:18-19), and speak glowingly about the sure hope in Christ that serves as an anchor for our souls. But if you are plagued by chronic despair that results in a "Why bother?" attitude, then prayerfully consider what you are about to read. Perhaps you will develop a perspective of hope rooted in the truth of God's amazing grace and will be able to put into place the first building block for moving toward oneness.

But remember that the Lord has not promised to put your marriage together for you. The hope of the Christian is *not* that one's spouse will change or that one's health will improve or that one's financial situation will become good. God does not promise to rearrange our worlds to suit our longings. He does promise to permit only those events that will further His purpose in our lives. Our responsibility is to respond to life's events in a manner intended to please the Lord, not to change our spouses into what we want. And if we do respond biblically, we have no guarantee that our spouses will respond in kind. Though they file for divorce or continue to drink or nag all the more, yet there is reason for us to persevere in obedience.

Certainly if *both* partners build on the foundation of hope and strive earnestly to live biblically, even the worst marriage can be turned around. Either way, there is reason to hope. This reason is bound up in the truth of the grace of God.

THE PRESENCE OF GOD

Notice a curious phrase in Matthew 26:65. Our Lord was on trial before the high priest of Israel. He had just demanded that Christ state clearly whether He was the Son of God. When the Lord affirmed His deity, Caiaphas, the high priest, immediately *tore his robes.* Why? What did his action signify?

Scripture records many instances when people tore their clothing. Joshua and Caleb tore their clothes when the Israelites refused to believe that God could give victory in Canaan (Num. 14:6). Jephthah tore his clothes when his daughter was the first to greet him when he returned home from battle, for he had made a hasty, ill-formed vow (Judg. 11). Barnabas and Paul tore their clothes when the citizens of Lystra reacted to a miracle by worshiping them as gods (Acts 14:11-14).

Other examples could be cited, but these are sufficient to make the point. Tearing one's clothing was a way of expressing grief and distress. The unbelief of the Jews at Kadesh-Barnea, the personal tragedy of sacrificing one's own daughter, and the false worship of men were regarded by Joshua, Jephthah, and Paul as terrible enough to provoke them into tearing their robes.

It is striking to notice that God specifically commanded that one group of people should never tear their robes because of distressing circumstances. The law given by Moses contained specific instructions that allowed a priest of God to rend his clothing only in the presence of blasphemy. God gave directions for sewing the priest's robes in a way that decreased the possibility of an accidental tear (Exod. 28:32; 39:23; Lev. 21:10). Only one factor could compel Caiaphas to tear his robe at Jesus' trial, and it was not personal grief over difficult circumstances.

When two of Aaron's sons were killed by the Lord as judgment for sin, Moses quickly told Aaron: ". . . Do not tear your clothes, or you will die" (Lev. 10:6). For someone who was not a priest to tear his robes would have been entirely appropriate on a sad occasion such as the death of his children. But for Aaron, a priest of God, it would be sin. Why? Why could Josiah the king tear his robes and thereby move God to pour out His blessing (2 Chron. 34:27-28)? Why would Aaron have been killed had he torn his robes? Why were kings and other leaders allowed to tear their robes without penalty (and often with blessing) when priests were not permitted to tear theirs?

The answer lies in a privilege accorded only to priests. In Old Testament times, only priests were permitted access into the tabernacle's Holy Place and, once a year, the high priest entered the Holy of Holies, the very presence of Jehovah. None but the high priest knew what it was to stand in that presence. None but the high priest could sprinkle the blood of the sacrificial lamb on the mercy seat to avert the righteous judgment of a holy God. Only he could approach God in this way and live.

Now, compare his privilege of access with his responsibility not to tear his robes. Recall that tearing robes was a cultural way of expressing profound despair over a disaster. The lesson is clear: Someone who has access to the immediate presence of God never has reason to regard anything as a disaster.

We can express this truth another way. When a person is aware of God's presence in his life, nothing that happens need provoke a sense of despair. If a priest were to tear his robes for personal grief, he would implicitly affirm that life presents problems for which God has no solutions. And that is never true. The God who is love, the God of eternity, the infinite, personal God who at once lives in the hearts of His people and sovereignly directs the flow of history is sufficient for every situation. Nothing takes him by surprise. No problem is beyond His power to master. There is no possible event in life for which His grace is not sufficient. People who can approach this God directly must not despair. To do so implies that God is impotent to work for eternal good in our set of circumstances.

One of the most remarkable truths revealed to the New Testament believer is that every member of the body of Christ is a priest (1 Peter 2:5). We are warmly encouraged to come boldly to the throne of God, to approach Him with the confidence that He understands our problems, sympathizes with our struggles, and is adequate to work through our circumstances for His purposes and our blessing. Because you and I as redeemed saints enjoy the privileged position of priests, we must never tear our robes. We must never regard any situation as bad enough to justify despair.

When events in our lives seem devastating and frustrating, we are invited to exercise our priestly right and approach the mercy seat of God. The choice is ours: Tear our robes in despair and make it our top priority to find relief from our pain, or depend so completely on the grace of God that we steadfastly refuse to compromise our commitment to live for the Lord.

Amazing grace! We deserve to endure the consequences of every sin we have ever committed, to suffer the loss of all that is good. Instead we are provided with the resources of our Great High Priest, who pleads our case before the divine Judge—and we are acquitted. Not only are we declared justified, but we are awarded the eternal care and protection of the Judge Himself. The holy Judge steps out from behind the bench and reveals Himself as our Loving Father.

Now, reconsider the question at the beginning of this chapter. What are we as husbands and wives to do when our marriage relationship has soured beyond any reasonable hope of sweetening? Are we to *tear our clothes* by resigning ourselves to the living martyrdom of enduring a spouse "till death do us part"? Should we *rip apart our garments* by escaping through divorce the awful ruin of our marriage? Are we to *cut up our suits and dresses* by seeking the companionship of someone more fulfilling to us than our partners? Or are we to regard these alternatives as unworthy and unbecoming for a priest of the almighty Shepherd. In His presence, there is never cause for despair. There may be pain or hurt or sadness, but never despair. Our spouses may not do what they should to restore our marriage to happy, fulfilling relationships. But if we remain faithful to God, pouring out our emotions before Him, renewing our commitment to seek Him, trusting Him to guide us in our responses, then He will sustain us through our trials and provide rich fellowship with Him. There is reason to go on. There is hope. God's grace is sufficient.

Perhaps your spouse will not join you on the path to oneness. But you can maintain your commitment—first to obey God and then to minister to your spouse through each opportunity that arises. The result will *possibly* be a better marriage (and in many cases *probably*). The result will *surely* be a new level of spiritual maturity and fellowship with Christ for you. And that is reason enough never to tear your robes.

The conclusion of the matter is this: In our pursuit of marital oneness, we must never permit failure or disappointment or tragedy to rob us of our confidence that God *can* heal our marriage and that He *will* deepen our maturity. No situation is so desperate that God's grace is not sufficient. Building a Christian marriage begins with a conscious confidence that a determination to live for God will result in something good. This confidence depends entirely on the first building block of marriage: The sufficient Grace of God.

7

Building Block 2:
COMMITMENT

The second building block of an effective marriage fits snugly atop of the first. If our confidence in God's grace is sufficient to maintain hope when despair seems justified, then we are in a position to commit ourselves to doing whatever God says. We can act on the strength of our hope by persisting to work on our marriages even when tempted to quit.

If we deeply believe that the Lord is able to work on our behalf in all circumstances, then no collection of marital setbacks will prompt us to seriously consider divorce or withdrawal.[1] If God is really as powerful as He claims to be, then the path of obedience will always lead to His intended purposes. The hope (better, the certainty) that God is at work to accomplish His plan even in the most difficult of marriages must remain firmly rooted in our awareness of His powerful grace—and that is Building Block 1.

If we further believe that not only is He at work, but that His purposes are always good, then from the depths of our being we will want—really *want*—to go His way. For the Christian who is keenly sensitive to the reality of God's goodness, obedience will not be experienced as forced compliance, but will reflect a freely chosen though sometimes painful surrender to a good plan. After counting the cost, the *decision* to obey will be supported by a *desire* to obey. This is Building Block 2: A deep desire to obey God by honoring the marriage commitment, a desire growing naturally out of the conviction that God is good.

---

[1]Many believe that the Bible permits a believer to regard certain behaviors on the part of a spouse (adultery and desertion) as legitimate basis for divorce. See Jay Adams's book *Marriage, Divorce and Remarriage* (Grand Rapids: Baker Book House, 1981) for a careful study of the subject. Regardless of circumstances, however, God's grace is sufficient to sustain the Christian in the path of obedience, which may include living alone.

Obedience to biblical direction, however, is too often regarded as an unwelcome and sometimes positively offensive duty, especially in marriage. When a man is married to a woman who incessantly complains, withholds affection, or reliably points out his social errors, the instruction to "love your wife" will seem more like an invitation to step on a nail than to enjoy a good meal. A woman whose husband justifies selfishness and insensitive demands under the banner of biblical teaching on headship will likely regard submission as an opportunity to lose her identity through demeaning subjection.

Something is terribly wrong when God's directions seem no more appealing than the harsh demands of an uncaring despot. Why do we sometimes respond to biblical instruction with a reluctant attitude of "doing one's duty" much as a recruit responds to the sergeant's command to get out of bed and do fifty push-ups? Why is there not a warm and confident anticipation as we follow the Lord, even when the path is steep and rocky?

Perhaps we misunderstand His instructions about loving our wives and submitting to our husbands and therefore try to do what He never required. Part of the problem may be traced to our sin-stained natures that stubbornly tend to see good as bad and bad as good.

Whatever the reasons behind our sometimes deplorable attitude toward obedience, one thing is certain. If we honor our commitment to be husbands and wives in a spirit of reluctant surrender or grudging compliance, we are not honoring our commitment at all. Imagine someone responding to a mission's appeal by saying, "All right, all right, you've done your job. I feel guilty. I've heard enough stories about starving natives and hell-bound pagans—I'll go if I have to. Where do I sign up?" What kind of missionary would this person be?

Scores of husbands and wives react to their marital obligations with just such an attitude. They make dreadful partners. Building Block 2 does *not* consist of obedience to God's will as an unwelcome duty. Certainly we are a people under authority, and we are bound to do what God commands. It is our duty. But obedience is so much more than mere duty. It is a privilege, an opportunity to enter into a depth of joy that makes every other pleasure seem shallow.

Why, then, do the commands to love our wives and submit to our husbands sometimes seem like a parent's order to come in from play and work on homework in our least favorite subject? In this chapter, we examine how we can genuinely *desire* to fulfill our marriage commitments, even when it requires us to minister to a disagreeable spouse.

Three concepts are essential to this purpose:

Point 1: The indispensable basis for an enduring, unwavering, and joyful commitment to obey all God's commands is implicit faith in the goodness of God;

Point 2: Obedience that develops from an awareness of God's goodness will be subjectively experienced as the pursuit of one's deepest desires rather than surrender to a duty;

Point 3: If there is no joy in honoring the marriage commitment, the fault does not lie in one's spouse, no matter how disagreeable he or she may be; the reason for lack of joy can be traced to a deficient awareness of the goodness of God.

Point 1: The basis for true commitment is the goodness of God.

Christian marriage counselors usually define love more in terms of actions and decisions than feelings. We know God's love because He *did* something, not because He *felt* something. We are often exhorted to love our spouses whether we feel like it or not. People who report that they no longer love their mates are urged to engage in a series of loving behaviors with the implicit promise that loving feelings will follow.

The correct assumption behind this thinking is that the truth of God's Word is to be the basis for our actions. We are not to be led by our erratic emotions, but are to follow biblical instruction whether our feelings agree or rebel.

God displayed His love with unmistakable clarity in what He *did*, but it is equally clear that these actions were accompanied by compassionate emotions. Not only did He *do* something for me, He also *felt* something for me. In the Book of Hosea, for example, God speaks of His heart breaking over the rebellion and unfaithfulness of His people, whom He tenderly characterizes over and over as His wife. The love of God includes feelings as well as behavior. In the same way, our commitment to love our spouses must generate more than lifeless, mechanical actions; there must be fervency about our behavior. But how does it develop?

The usual argument promises that loving feelings flow from loving behavior: If we do enough loving deeds for someone for a long enough period of time, eventually we will feel loving emotions for that person. But one weakness in this reasoning is that it does not deal with a core problem: Many husbands and wives simply do not *want* to be loving toward their mates. A forceful pastor or counselor may push the person to do what should be done, but the marriage will likely not improve.

This leaves us with a dilemma. If we must *want* to love our spouses with a subjective desire to do so, and if *doing* loving things will not generate that desire, how are we to come by it? The choice seems to be between mechanical niceness or passionate withdrawal. Perhaps we are to wait for the Holy Spirit to inflame our insides. Exactly what is an indifferent husband or wife to do?

Listen in on a typical counseling session

Husband: "I just can't love that woman."

Counselor: "If love is defined as a willingness to sacrificially minister to your wife, then you *can* love her. You can say kind words, express affection, extend courtesies."

Husband: "But it would all be so empty. Sure I can do it! But I would feel phony and dishonest, like I was faking. I don't feel warm at all toward her."

Counselor: "So you *can* do it, but because you don't *feel* it, you *won't* do it. Is that correct?

Husband: "Look, there's just no point! It isn't real! I just don't want to love that woman. Do you know what she did this past week? She . . ."

Notice the assumption governing this man's thinking: The *desire* to honor his marriage commitment depends essentially on the attitudes and actions of his spouse. Simply put, "If my partner is nice to me, I *can desire* to be nice to her. If she is not nice to me, then I *cannot desire* to be nice to her. Perhaps I can do what I should, but I cannot *want* to do what I should. The most that I can muster is a resigned willingness to obey God by continuing to walk through this dark valley of my marriage. I suppose I can do what God commands, but don't expect me to *want* to be loving and kind. It just isn't possible to desire to love someone who treats you the way my spouse treats me."

If marriage counselors assign this husband the task of "behaving warmly" toward his wife when he feels nothing but indifference or coldness, they are doing the marriage no great favor. More needs to be done. For the relationship to reflect the Christ-church union properly, there needs to be a keenly felt desire to minister lovingly to one's spouse. But how do we stir up that godly desire when it simply isn't there and when our partners continue to pour water on the already flameless altar?

Is the solution a matter of "doing it until you feel it"? Let me begin to answer the problem with an illustration.

When I was in the second grade, I dropped the end of a bench I was carrying on the big toe of my right foot. The nail split, blood spurted, and I howled. Within minutes that seemed like hours, I was lying flat on our family doctor's table with my mother, who had been called by the school, standing by my side. The physician—unruffled sort who reacted to cries of anguish by slowly stroking his chin—examined the toe, then reached for a needle. When I realized he intended to stick the needle into my toe, I panicked. I felt no desire whatsoever to be stabbed by that needle.

Helplessly I looked up at my mother, and she was smiling, not a happy smile, but an encouraging "be brave" sort of smile. Now, a woman who smiled in that situation was either a heartless sadist *or* a loving mother who wanted her son to know that somehow the horror of the moment was a necessary part of a good plan. I knew my mother. I had lived with her for seven years and had adequate reason to believe that she was for me, not against me.

With that realization fixed in my mind, her steady smile produced in me the *desire* to submit to a difficult and painful course of action—to lie still. I was not entirely persuaded of the doctor's kind intentions—at the moment he still seemed dangerous—but I had absolute confidence in mother's goodness. From that confidence came a genuine willingness to commit myself to whatever course of action she approved, knowing that her goodness was my guarantee of eventual satisfaction with the outcome. My *desire* to do something unpleasant depended entirely on my awareness of the character of the person who wanted me to do it.

Many husbands and wives judge their marriages (sometimes with excellent reason) as no more pleasant than having a long needle inserted daily into a wounded big toe. Why sit still for it? Why not get up and walk out? Separation from the source of additional pain makes perfect sense if the goal is immediate relief. People suffering intense pain naturally have one overriding desire: to feel less pain. Whatever provides instant relief is seen as desirable; whatever makes pain worse is seen as undesirable. When people are in pain, they earnestly want whatever brings relief. And nothing is abnormal about that. To bang my head against the wall when I already have a headache would be evidence of mental disorder, not of a noble willingness to suffer.

Yet God seems to counter this sensible thinking when He requires husbands and wives to honor commitments that only create more hurt.

Without a thorough confidence that God would never ask His

children to do anything that does not have their well-being in view, we simply will not be able to arouse a desire to honor the commitment of marriage. And that is as it should be. It makes no sense to follow the directions of a guide whose motivation you do not trust.

Our failure to readily follow His leading reflects a lack of deep confidence in His goodness. We wonder whether He is merely using us or wants to bless us. The problem with unsteady commitment is not centrally a problem of the *will*; it is rather deficient *belief*. We simply do not believe that the God who tells us to remain committed to our marriage partners is good. If we *knew* He was good, we would sense a deep desire to follow His leading in the same spirit with which I responded to mother's smiling encouragement to let the doctor stick my toe.

It follows that the basic cure for weak commitment is *renewed faith, not rededicated effort*. Urgings to "love your wife and submit to your husband whether you feel like it or not" fail to lay the axe to the root of the problem. Unless God's goodness is clearly established as the context for obedience, such exhortations will at best keep the weeds of anger and dissension from spreading. They will not expose and rip out the hidden, flourishing root system whose flower is the ugly growth of broken promises. Exhortation to obedience is important and right. But the framework of God's goodness must be understood if the prompting is to be gladly obeyed.

The wife of an alcoholic or preoccupied workaholic; the husband of an icy bed-partner; a square-jawed drill sergeant—any of these will profit less from a lecture on commitment than from a deepened awareness of God's goodness. The two go hand in hand: Obedience to God's orders deepens our awareness of His goodness, and our awareness of His goodness provides motivation for further obedience. Obedience without an awareness of His goodness produces a labored commitment that robs us of joy. An awareness of God's goodness that is not coupled with obedience is shallow and will become lifelessly academic.

It makes sense to honor our marriage commitments because the God who tells us to do so is a good God who wants our best. The path He is marking out for us leads to unparalleled joy for us and glory for Him. An awareness of His character naturally stimulates a desire to follow His leading.

Point 2: Honoring commitments because of a profound trust in God's goodness will feel less like "doing one's duty" and more like pursuing ones deepest desires.

If a starving man were asked to feed his hungry neighbor, he would understandably be less than eager to obey. If he could lay his hands on food, he would want to eat it himself. To give something away that we desperately crave is not easy. To *want* to give it away seems ridiculous and impossible.

In marriage, it sometimes seems that we are asked to give up all hopes for personal happiness in order to provide happiness for our mates. A husband recently told me in front of his tearful wife: "I know she wants me to call off the divorce, but I'm convinced that I simply cannot be happy with her. You're asking me to forget about my fulfillment so that my wife can be spared the pain of divorce. I'm sorry, but when it comes down to my happiness or hers, I'm just not willing to be a martyr."

I wonder how many of us, perhaps unwittingly, view God's direction for marriage in a similar light. It seems that when we place greater priority on our spouses' happiness than on our own, somehow we are the losers. Note that if we retain this attitude, we will remain faithful to our marriage vows up to the point of diminishing returns; that is, as long as giving to our spouse brings us what we want, we will gladly keep our promises. The moment the choice becomes our happiness or theirs, the marriage commitment will feel like a prison keeping us locked away from freedom and joy. If we choose to honor it, we will necessarily do so in a spirit of "doing our time."

Consider the following typical dialogue:

Counselor:	"Can you see that your marriage presents you with a unique opportunity to really minister to the needs of your husband?"
Wife:	"Yes, I know what you mean—that I should try to build him up so he can feel better about himself. I've tried for years to do that. It really hasn't helped much, but I'll keep trying."
Counselor:	"Why?"
Wife:	"Why what?"
Counselor:	"Why will you keep on trying to minister to him?"
Wife:	"Because I know I should."
Counselor:	"What I hear you saying is that you'll keep trying because it's your duty. But your heart really isn't in it. You don't really want to."
Wife:	"No, I really don't."
Counselor:	"Then I see very little reason to try."

At this point, the puzzled wife is wondering whether I as the counselor am advocating divorce or perhaps separation. I am in fact suggesting no such thing. She should submit to her husband and work hard in her ministry to him, but unless at some deep level she desires to be a good wife, her efforts will amount to no more than the mechanical rehearsal of an imposed script. And that does not add up to being a good wife.

We might ask why a wife would *want* to minister to an irritating, cold, rejecting husband. Pressured compliance to biblical demand is not enough. Consider again the starving man who has a hungry neighbor. Suppose you were to assure him that a banquet had been specially prepared for him. As a promise of good things to come, you gave him a generous appetizer of shrimp cocktail and a sampling from a perfectly prepared prime rib of beef. Imagine further that you assured him that there was plenty for everyone. As he looked across the fence to his pale, emaciated neighbor, assume that what struck him most was his neighbor's need and that this stark awareness eclipsed all memories of previous squabbles about borrowed lawn mowers and noisy parties.

Carry the fantasy one step further. Suppose the provider of the feast asked this man to carry a slice of beef to his neighbor and invite him to come along for the meal. Would he respond with, "Well, I don't want to, but I guess it's only right. Oh, O.K., I'll do it"? Or would he gladly run next door with the good news that food is available, willing and eager to share his bit of beef to persuade his neighbor to join him for the banquet?

Christian marriage, viewed in the context of God's provision and our needs, is much like this parable. All my needs are completely met in Christ. The riches of heaven are mine. I am called to believe this. And God has given me a taste of what lies ahead to excite my faith. The problem, sadly, is that very few Christians have really tasted and seen that the Lord is good. The joy of fellowship with Christ and service in His name is less than a thrilling reality for too many Christians because of inadequate commitment to Him. But those who have cast their entire lot with Christ know something of the joy and peace He provides.

God also commands me to share with others what He has given me. With the clear eyesight of one whose hunger has been satisfied, partly now and fully in prospect, I can see beneath whatever offends me in my wife to the needs she has for the same food I am enjoying. My heart is moved with compassion. I find compelling desire to be God's instrument in creating hope within her for the full satisfaction of her hunger.

Let me summarize this in a sentence: If I have experienced the answer to my deepest longings in Christ, then I will be able to see past my longings and discern my wife's needs; and when I see her needs, then my experience of satisfaction with Christ will create in me a deep desire to promote similar satisfaction in my wife.

Does this theorizing sound elegant and far removed from the realities of everyday bickering? The very fact that it strikes us as beyond the reach of normal life is testimony to how far beneath the normal *Christian* life we usually live. It is normal for Christians to taste and see that God is good. Then, convinced of His goodness and satisfied with His plan for our lives, we are to regard ourselves as instruments of ministry. A proper understanding of marriage as a calling to high ministry will cause us to look at the deepest needs of our mates and to appreciate our unique opportunity to touch those needs in significant ways.

Because we are not experiencing the satisfaction that comes from resting in God's goodness, we look to our partners to meet our needs. When they fail to do so, as inevitably they will, we retreat behind protective distance to minimize our discomfort. But, because we are "Bible-believing Christians," we nobly carry on with the responsibilities of marriage in a spirit of obedient martyrdom, persuaded that God admires our devotion to duty.

Christians who have put God to the test by vulnerably surrendering to His will, examining their motives regularly to see where they are protecting themselves rather than ministering, are tasting the goodness of God. These people more and more see their marriage commitment as an opportunity to pursue their deepest desires, to follow a good path and to invite their spouses to walk with them. Their marital vows are not regarded as a depressing duty to fulfill.

Point 3: Lack of joy in honoring the marriage commitment cannot be blamed on our spouses; the fault lies in our failure to depend on the goodness of God.

The third point flows naturally from the first two. No attitude is more stubborn than our blaming the lack of spiritual fruit on someone or something else. The Scriptures plainly state that joy is the product of the Holy Spirit's work in our lives as we yield ourselves to His control. Yet, when an irritation or discouragement blocks our joy, our minds immediately recite how someone else has failed us.

In a mood of unwitting self-righteousness, we remind ourselves (and our counselors) of all the things we must endure. Behind this focus on our mates' faults is a subtle, unbiblical assumption: Our lack of joy can be blamed on our spouses. If only he or she would change, then I could enjoy my role as a loving husband or submissive wife. Joy is seen as the fruit of the partner's attitudes and behavior, not as the fruit of the Spirit.

It is true that much of my subjective happiness depends on how my wife treats me. I have a wife who loves and respects me, and I thoroughly enjoy her warmth and support. Because of her attitude toward me, I am able to honor my commitment to love her with a certain ease and delight. If she were to turn on me, I have no doubt that my promise to love her as Christ loved the church would be severely tested. Even if I were to lean so heavily on God that I continued to faithfully minister as a loving husband, the gladness that characterized my ministry before she turned against me would be greatly diminished or eliminated.

Where, then, is my joy? If it is gone, am I not justified in attributing its loss to my wife's change in attitude? If I developed a defeated, joyless spirit as I worked at maintaining my commitment to love her, could I not blame my wife for my lack of joy?

Although the tingling pleasure of embracing a responsive wife would be gone, the loss of joy in my marital ministry would reflect on my reduced confidence that God's plan for my life was good. As long as this plan includes a loving wife, I have little difficulty believing in His goodness. But when He calls me to love a rejecting woman, it requires herculean faith to continue believing that His plan is good. If I do continue in that confidence, however, the essential joy of ministry remains.

The missionary whose efforts God rewards with many converts returns to his home church beaming with enthusiastic reports of God's blessing. The missionary whose equally faithful efforts yield no apparent fruit cannot feel the same quality of excitement. But he need not return hanging his head. Although the pain of discouragement is real and can provoke spiritual struggle and self-examination, the faithful servant of God has reason for joy in the guarantee that every act of obedience done for the sake of Christ is accomplishing its intended purpose and brings a smile to the lips of the Savior.

I confess that I would much prefer to be the missionary with a booming ministry, just as I am glad to be the husband of a loving wife. But whether blessed with pleasant circumstances or tested by painful trial, the Christian's final basis for joy remains the same: The confidence that our faithfulness pleases Christ and is used by

Him according to His sovereign plan. Because His plan is good, obedience brings joy to the sincere Christian.

Several couples who recently sat in my office shook their heads as I discussed these concepts with them. This teaching is hard. It is no easy matter to build (or rebuild) your marriage on the conviction that God's grace is sufficient reason for continued obedience (Building Block 1) and for honoring your vows consistently in the conviction that God's plan is always good (Building Block 2).

The difficulty lies in part in the failure to comprehend that God is able: we become discouraged with problems and quit working. Another part of the problem is our limited and wavering awareness that God is good: we lose any real desire to follow His directions.

But some of the resistance to joyful and persistent ministry may be attributed to a confusion on what to do with conflicts in our marriage relationships. This brings us to the third building block, the subject of the next chapter.

8

Building Block 3:
ACCEPTANCE

Before we summon the building inspector to evaluate our marital structure, another building block needs to be positioned atop the first two.

A frustrated husband I know seemed to grasp the concepts of grace and commitment readily, but he still faced a dilemma. "I'm convinced," he said, "that God is perfectly capable of turning any apparent catastrophe into a means of blessing. This belief has kept me from throwing in the towel with my marriage. I also am aware that God is good and that His plan is good. So I really do want to follow His directions for my life as a husband.

"But I'll be honest with you! You've helped me a lot to see these ideas about sufficient grace and desired commitment, but sometimes my wife really gets to me. She does so many things that just plain annoy me. I think they'd annoy anyone. Our bedroom is never picked up, the dishes are stacked in the sink for days, she is busy running around taking food to sick neighbors and attending women's Bible studies, and she rarely listens to me. She usually gives me advice with a few Bible verses thrown in.

"I've tried my best to handle it well. I really have! I've been patient, I offered to get her help with the housework, I've tried not to criticize, I've cleaned up the kitchen myself many times without grumbling, I've bought her thoughtful gifts—but I've just about had it! After working all day in a pressure-cooker job, I don't need to walk into a messy house wondering if I'll get a decent dinner.

"If I'm supposed to feel some sort of warm acceptance of her, then I'm in trouble—because I don't! At one level I sincerely want to minister to her and I'm honestly trying; but at another level she's driving me crazy! What am I supposed to do with all my frustration?"

No matter how intimate their relationship or firm their commitment, all married people find their mates annoying or maddening at times. So how is one to *accept*, not just endure, an ill-mannered or irritating spouse? The concepts of God's grace and goodness do not provide an adequate answer.

The Bible requires that we do more, far more, than tolerate one another. We are instructed to accept each other as God accepts us (Rom. 15:7). We are to forbear one another in love, and this involves something different from putting up with our mates with a resigned sigh (Eph. 4:32); we are to evidence the spiritual fruit of love, patience, and kindness (Gal. 5:22). Christian relationships must include more than a willingness to remain involved because of God's sustaining grace. They require more than an earnest commitment to minister to each other. Somehow we are supposed to accept one another.

We must see clearly that acceptance requires us to go beyond a desire to minister. The missionary tending a leper could continue in a most unpleasant ministry on the strength of a deep commitment to God and to needy people. But to accept the one who is so unattractively ill is quite another matter, especially if the leper has an ungrateful, bitter spirit.

What does a husband do when his wife is the church bore, when at every social gathering of the church the saints scurry to avoid listening to her endless chatter? What does it mean to accept a tiresome wife?

Consider the plight of a refined woman whose husband shovels food from plate to mouth in one continuous motion, pausing only when he needs time to clear some space for the next forkful. Although she may successfully struggle to keep her commitment to her graceless partner, she can scarcely be faulted for feeling embarrassed and perturbed.

The everyday realities of living with an imperfect partner make the work of accepting one another sometimes a severe test. Yet Christian marriage requires a thorough, sincere, and substantially felt acceptance of the other no matter what disagreeable habits make the task difficult.

So let's examine what it means to add *acceptance* (Building Block 3) to *grace* and *commitment* (Building Blocks 1 and 2). We will begin with two central points.

> Point 1: There is a difference between *accepting* your mate and *enjoying* your mate; the former is a requirement, the latter is a blessing;

Point 2: The experience of accepting your spouse depends upon the work of forgiveness, which in turn depends upon a willingness to see the offensive behavior of your spouse in biblical context.

Point 1: The difference between accepting and enjoying.

Nothing is more crucial to our marriage-building efforts than a realistic evaluation of where we are. Only when we admit a problem will we search for a solution.

Because God is able to handle whatever problems exist, we must never deny the problems we face. Marriage sometimes includes living with an infuriating, unpleasant, disappointing, or obnoxious person. It will not advance our efforts to create greater oneness in marriage if we quietly skirt these experiences by focusing on our partner's good points or reminding ourselves that we should be kind.

Every marriage has its tense moments when one spouse frustrates the other, sometimes seriously and sometimes not so seriously. We must therefore understand what it means to accept a frustrating spouse.

As a first step toward finding the answer, consider what happens when we are offended. At least two distinguishable responses can be identified: a *decision* and an *emotion.*

When our mates annoy or disappoint us, we can consciously decide whether to remain committed to ministry or to retreat behind self-protective maneuvering. The natural reaction is a desire to reduce pain and to avoid similar events. We may flow with our impulses and pursue a course intended to make us more comfortable (or less uncomfortable), or we may consciously choose the goal of continued ministry regardless of personal cost. The decision before us is to *manipulate* with our needs in view or to *minister* with our partner's needs in view.

Our second response to an interpersonal event is emotional. We *feel* something. If the event is affirming and kind, we feel good; if the event is threatening and cruel, we feel bad. Whether we experience pleasant or unpleasant emotions depends entirely on the nature of the event. It is not a matter of choice. I cannot *choose* to feel warm if my wife insults me; nor can I *choose* to feel happy when she pays me a compliment. Feelings are not directly the result of a choice, but a natural response to a situation.

This point must be clear. Regardless of how much we consciously choose to entrust our deepest personal needs to God's care

(Spirit Oneness) and despite a determination to minister to our mates (Soul Oneness), unpleasant events still generate unpleasant emotions.[1] Jesus wept at Lazarus' death. But He, with the angels, rejoiced at Zacchaeus' conversion. The nature of the event determined the type of emotion.

In general terms, events trigger one of two primary emotions. Whatever specific feelings we experience fit more or less within the basic emotional categories of *enjoyment* or *displeasure*. Some events prompt little emotional response; for example, I feel neither enjoyment nor displeasure when my wife purchases a new toothbrush. My concern lies not with those relatively emotionless events, but with the many actions that provoke a discernible emotional response.

Let us label a person's behavior toward his or her spouse an *event*, some concrete action of which the other is aware that does generate an emotional reaction. Remember that whether we feel enjoyment or displeasure in response to the event is determined entirely by the nature of the event. It follows that we bear no responsibility for which feeling we experience.

James' admonition to "consider it pure joy . . . whenever you face trials" (James 1:2) does not mean that spiritual people feel no pain when they encounter rejection. God has formed us as social beings with interpersonal nerve endings. When someone kicks me in the leg, I should feel pain; if I feel nothing, something is wrong with my leg. In the same way, if I experience rejection as pleasurable, something is wrong with my psyche. It is senseless for a woman to feel guilty over being displeased when her husband is harshly critical of her. To feel good when rejected is not evidence of spiritual character, but of psychological disorder or contrived piety.

My first point can be simply stated: We respond to the event of a spouse's behavior both with a *decision* to minister or manipulate (which depends entirely on personal choice) and with an *emotion* of enjoyment or displeasure (which depends entirely on the nature of the event).

Notice that the decision involves an action that moves *toward the event* and the emotion is a response that comes *from the event.*

---

[1]Some popular thinking today regards all events as thoroughly neutral. In this view, events become unpleasant or pleasant exclusively through our *defining* them so. Such a position assumes that we live in a meaningless, amoral world. To the Christian, this idea is unacceptable. In a world created and governed by a personal God who has definite character, events that reflect His character are good, and events that contradict His character are bad. An act of love is a pleasant event because God is love; an act of hate is unpleasant because it violates God's character.

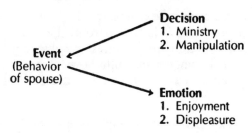

Figure 1

When couples hear the speaker at a marriage seminar instruct them to accept one another, I wonder how many assume they are responsible to feel enjoyment every moment they are with their mates. Yet, when your spouse treats you badly, displeasure is normal and inevitable. If acceptance requires the feeling of enjoyment, it is impossible to accept a husband or wife who treats you badly.

If husbands equate acceptance with enjoyment, they likely drive away from the seminar informing their wives that if they would just behave more agreeably, accepting them would be no problem. Wives, I suppose, would respond with similar sentiment. When accepting one's spouse is confused with enjoying one's spouse, each partner blames the other for the lack of acceptance (meaning enjoyment) in the marriage.

The Bible requires that we accept our mates. Apparently God assumes that we are able to *accept* a partner whom we do not *enjoy*. Acceptance must differ from enjoyment. I am somehow capable of accepting my partner whether her behavior occasions enjoyment or displeasure. If my mate treats me kindly, I may legitimately regard the *enjoyment* I feel as a blessing. But whether my spouse provokes enjoyment or displeasure, I am to regard my *acceptance* of her as a requirement. If acceptance has nothing to do with our *emotional response* of enjoyment or displeasure, what does it involve?

It may seem obvious that acceptance is tied up with our *decision* to minister rather than to manipulate, and that we are free to minister to even the most displeasurable spouse if we so choose. But accepting one's spouse involves more than the decisive commitment to minister. It is possible to remain unreserving in a choice to minister without in fact accepting one's spouse. Sincere ministry can be carried on with a certain reserve that maintains a distance between the minister and the object of ministry. Something indefinable that clearly obstructs a deep oneness is present in the relationship. There is a lack of acceptance.

If acceptance cannot be defined as the basic *emotions* we feel toward our spouses, and if it goes beyond the *decision* to remain steadfast in our commitment to minister, what does it mean to accept someone? To understand fully how to accept a sometimes displeasurable partner, we must consider the biblical concept of forgiveness.

Point 2: The experience of accepting a spouse depends on the work of forgiveness, which in turn depends upon a willingness to see the offensive behavior of the spouse in biblical context.

Mary offends Bill. Bill *feels* displeasure, but reaffirms his *decision* to minister to her despite her offensive behavior. Yet something is missing. Bill knows it and Mary soon will. Although he desires to minister because he wants to obey God, his efforts to be loving seem mechanical. He is aware of a strange pressure to minister that reduces his husbandly actions to a piece of theater, like becoming someone else for the sake of the script.

As he prays about this unnaturalness in his approach to Mary, Bill senses bitterness within that intensifies whenever he relives in his mind what Mary has done to him. He realizes that his emotional attitude toward Mary effectively blocks any movement toward oneness. Bill therefore determines to rid himself of this anger so that he can truly accept Mary. But he cannot accept someone he resents. First he has to extinguish the flames of bitterness to permit the growth of a warm, unpressured willingness to minister, a desire to love his wife, based not only on God's goodness but also on his profound concern for his wife.

Bill turns to a Christian counselor for help. "How can I overcome my bitter spirit so my concern for Mary can grow out of deep acceptance of her?"

The counselor responds, "The reason you are still angry is that you have not yet forgiven Mary for her offense. The presence of bitterness indicates that the deep work of forgiveness has not really been accomplished."

Bill reflects on his counselor's advice and comes to see that forgiving Mary is a necessary step if he is truly to accept her.

Notice the definition of acceptance implied in this vignette: *To accept someone means that we minister to the person with no resentment or pressure to minister as we do so.* In other words, acceptance involves both channels of our response to an event: (1) the decision to minister; and (2) the absence of the feelings that interfere with ministry.

The first element is simply a choice to either minister or manipulate. The second element is complex. No one is able to "will away" bitter feelings on demand. Yet, to truly accept someone who has offended us, we must somehow be freed from the hostile emotions that the memory of the offense provokes. How can I become "unbitter" and thus accepting?

With characteristic simplicity, the Bible spells out the solution in a word. The shift from bitterness to benevolence, from forced kindness to freely given love, requires *forgiveness*. A precise understanding of what forgiveness entails and how the work of forgiveness roots out the weeds of resentment will be helpful. For this understanding we must examine the source of bitter feelings.

Think back to the discussion of our two basic personal needs, security and significance. Because our needs are fully met in relationship with Christ, we can approach life with the resources to give out of fullness. The freedom Christ provides includes the freedom to require nothing of our mates. We will hurt when a spouse rejects or disrespects us, but the Lord's love and purpose for us enable us to continue giving no matter how little we receive. It is possible, therefore, even with the most disagreeable of mates, to maintain our goal of ministry rather than to manipulate.

Nevertheless, no matter how much I may prattle on about needing nothing from my spouse, I continue to desire a great deal from her. I want companionship, emotional support, respect, appreciation, sexual fulfillment, and more. Because I desire certain responses from my mate, her offensive behavior has the power to hurt me and displease me. If I wanted nothing from her, then the withdrawal of her affections would occasion no pain. But I do want something from my wife, and I should. When I fail to receive what I want, I will necessarily feel displeasure. But how do hurt and displeasure deteriorate into bitterness?

In my earlier books on counseling I suggested that our *evaluation* of an event will in large measure determine our *specific feelings* about it.[2] An event occurs. If I *believe* that the event is a serious threat to my physical or personal well-being, I will *feel* deeply anxious and enraged about it. If, however, I am convinced that the event though painful involves no substantial damage to my person, I will feel unhappy and perhaps irritated but essentially untroubled. One example suffices to illustrate the principle.

When the doctor comes from the operating room with a

---

[2]*Basic Principles of Biblical Counseling* (Grand Rapids: Zondervan, 1975) and *Effective Biblical Counseling* (Grand Rapids: Zondervan, 1977).

somber frown, the waiting husband normally feels a fearful emptiness. But suppose a man had been involved in an adulterous affair and was hoping for an opportunity to end his marriage without embarrassment. The same event (a surgeon's frown) would then elicit a very different emotion, perhaps a measure of sadness mingled with relieved anticipation. The *specific* emotion is determined not by the event itself (the frown indicating his wife's death) but by what the event means to the husband (loss of a loved one vs. an opportunity to enter into a desired relationship more gracefully).

Although the nature of the event will determine whether the emotional response is positive or negative (enjoyment or displeasure), the evaluation of the event by the individual will influence the specific content and intensity of the emotional response.

Trace what happens when Bill is offended by Mary. Bill's immediate and necessary response is displeasure. Call this emotion the Primary Emotional Response.

As soon as the displeasurable event occurs, Bill will *evaluate* the event—often without conscious thought. He will perceive that the event is related either to his needs or to his desires. If Bill believes that his self-respect depends on Mary's approval, he will then incorrectly regard her offensive behavior as a real threat to his need for significance.

It is hoped that Bill has understood that Mary's behavior has no bearing whatever on his needs because Christ has proved Himself sufficient. If this belief is a deep conviction, Bill will be free from self-centered preoccupation with how Mary's offense made him feel. He would, of course, regard Mary's behavior as an unfortunate and painful denial of his *desires* and would feel some sadness.

Whether Bill becomes bitter will depend on his evaluation of the event. If he wrongly believes Mary's offense is a threat to his *needs*, then the Primary Emotional Response of displeasure will quickly shift into the Secondary Emotional Response of bitterness. But if he correctly perceives the events as a block to his *desires*, his displeasure will develop into the Secondary Emotional Response of sad, perhaps angry, *disappointment.* [3]

---

[3]The distinction between righteous anger and sinful anger is often poorly understood. If a careless driver scrapes my car in a parking lot, I will likely feel anger. If I can maintain the perspective that my goal even as I contemplate my damaged car is to glorify the Lord, then the anger that I feel will not be controlling or consuming. It will reflect the fact that a legitimate desire (to have a blemish-free car) has been blocked. My disappointment will certainly include an angry tone but, as I understand it, if my goal does not shift from pleasing God to getting revenge, then my anger is righteous; it will not interfere with achieving the purposes of God.

Imagine a very different event. Suppose Mary had thoughtfully surprised Bill with a special expression of her love. His Primary Emotional Response would be enjoyment. If he evaluated such acts of kindness as essential to his needs ("I need affirmation from my wife in order to know that I am respected"), the feeling of enjoyment would rapidly slip into the derivative feeling of *dependency*. However, if Bill, like Paul in Philippians 4, were grateful for extended kindness but maintained his dependency on the Lord, then his Secondary Emotional Response would become a warm, non-possessive *satisfaction*.

The discussion can be illustrated easily in these two diagrams:

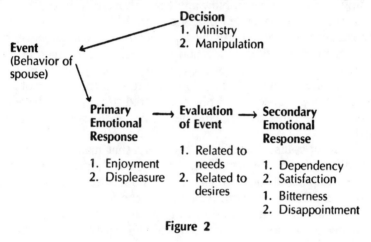

Figure 2

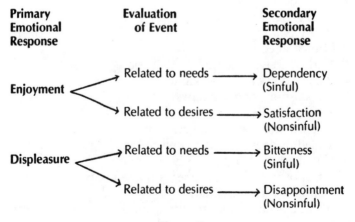

Figure 3

Now, with all these concepts secure in our minds, we are ready to explore the central idea of forgiveness. Luke 17 records Jesus' parable of a certain man forgiving another of a financial debt. This story illustrates the core meaning of forgiveness: the cancellation of a debt.

If I borrowed a hundred dollars from you, I am responsible to repay it to you. Satisfying the debt is my moral obligation. If for some reason, you elect to cancel or forgive the debt, then I am no longer required to pay you the borrowed sum. In effect, you bear the weight of my debt because you absorb the loss.

Forgiveness consists of not requiring payment from the offending or indebted party. Now apply this thought to interpersonal debts. When Mary offended Bill, she wronged him. She incurred a debt that can be satisfied only by experiencing just consequences of punishment and retribution. When Bill is asked to forgive her, he may say to himself—as many offended spouses do—something like this: "But she was wrong! Why do I have to bear the weight of her offense? It doesn't seem fair! She committed the sin and I have to let her off the hook by forgiving her? But she deserves to be punished!"

This, of course, is precisely the point that makes forgiveness both difficult and commendable. She deserves punishment. Forgiveness requires a most unnatural decision to demand that the offender experience no punitive consequence for wrongdoing.

To grasp what the decision to forgive really entails, think of the many retaliations an offended and unforgiving person could impose on his or her mate:

- Reminders of the offense
- Cold shoulder
- Angry pouting
- Cooled affection
- Withheld sex or dutiful participation
- Elimination of routine kindnesses
- Stubborn uncooperativeness
- Superior smiles
- Clipped and abrupt conversation
- Veiled or open threats to end the marriage
- Humiliation in front of others

and a host of others whose number is limited only by the creative imagination of a vengeful mind.

No counselor could hope to anticipate all the schemes scurrying about in the daydreams of an offended spouse. Forgiveness requires more than an agreement to end a checklist of retaliatory activities. The forgiving partner must be committed to requiring *no consequences at all* for the offense. There must be (1) a decision to forgive, followed by (2) a renewed commitment to minister, which then must (3) bear the fruit of extending kindness to the offending mate.

A resentful husband or wife who is struggling with accepting the other might conclude from the discussion so far that forgiveness requires *definite decisions* and *changed behaviors.* If forgiveness involves nothing more than these elements, we might sketch what it means to forgive as follows:

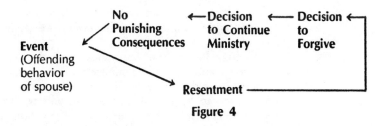

Figure 4

Suppose Bill, our offended husband who is still struggling to forgive Mary, tries to put this conception of forgiveness into practice. Will he find himself moving closer to a deeply experienced, warm *acceptance* of his wife? After sincere efforts to follow the program of choosing to forgive and to minister, I wonder if he might sense an incompleteness in his forgiveness, a biting edge to his attitude that would block a full, rich acceptance of his wife. Perhaps he would report a feeling of pressured, irritable obligation in carrying out his ministry.

"I can forgive my wife for what she did," Bill tells his counselor at their next meeting, "but I can't get it out of my mind. I am willing to keep on treating her well even though I don't feel especially warm toward her. Yes, I understand that my decision to forgive and to minister does not require a pool of warm feelings. But I can't keep my mind from thinking about what Mary did.

"And everytime I think of it," Bill continues, "I feel angry and upset all over again. Will those angry feelings fade away if I keep on working at treating her well? I cannot feel that I'm really accepting her as long as I'm still mad. But I just don't know what to do about my bitterness. My efforts to forgive her by deciding to forgive and choosing to minister have not really helped much with that problem."

If we are to help this frustrated husband genuinely accept his wife, we must expand his understanding of forgiveness. Is forgiveness defined entirely in terms of *decisions* to forgive and *choices* to minister? What are we to do with the angry emotions and pressure that persist despite our best efforts to put the offense out of our minds? Do we bury the memory each time it recurs, hoping that eventually we will forget it? Is it possible to really forget?

Many offended people meet with one of two responses when they ask these questions. The first response is wholly unsatisfactory, the second incomplete:

> *Response 1:* "God forgets our sins when He forgives us; we too can and must forget the offense of others when we forgive them."
>
> *Response 2:* "The continued practice of forgiveness (i.e., the decision to forgive and to continue ministering, requiring no consequences for the offense) will eventually enable the offended party to regard the offense as an unimportant piece of history that arouses no feelings at all; eventually the mind drops it from awareness as trivia."

In Jeremiah 31:34, Jehovah says, "For I will forgive their wickedness and will remember their sins no more." Some find in this verse support for Response 1, that real forgiveness includes forgetting. But the issue is not so easily resolved.

In all likelihood, the verse is not teaching that God literally forgets our sin in the same manner that an amnesia victim forgets his name. This sort of memory loss is no virtue; rather, it involves an inability to call a fact into awareness, a deficiency in mental functioning. But an omniscient mind has no blind spots.

The passage probably refers to the truth that our gracious God chooses to remember our sins *against us* no more, that is, He will not bring the matter up again. Because of the atoning work of Christ, God has canceled our debt and no longer requires payment. The debt has already been paid. This "forgetting" of our sins is inherent in my earlier statement: Forgiveness involves a willingness to release an offending party from all requirement to experience the just consequences of his wrongdoing. Advice to forget an offense in the sense in which God "forgets" our sin does not address the problem of feeling angry when the memory of the offense recurs. It goes no further than the counsel to decide to forgive and to choose to minister. The problem of bitter feelings remains untouched.

Counsel to forget an offense fails to advance our understanding of forgiveness, and it is also discouraging. If taken literally, such counsel insists that either we damage the memory storage area of our brains or we introduce selective amnesia through the process of pathological repression. Of course, no one is recommending these absurd remedies.

But some in the Christian community seem to imply that nailing down the lid on volcanoes of angry emotion by selective attention (choosing to think only about pleasant events) will solve the problem. It won't. Such effort serves only to deepen the bitterness and reroute its expression into avenues more subtly sinful than direct hostility. The result is often an assortment of physical aches and pains, increased irritability, impulsive eating, or any of innumerable other expressions of disowned anger.

What about the second response? Will the offense eventually be forgotten as easily as the memory of what we had for breakfast three days ago?

This counsel correctly aims toward stripping the troublesome memory of its power to elicit negative arousal. In my view, however, it fails to reach its goal. Does the continued practice of kind behavior toward an offending person, even if done with a firm decision to be forgiving, eventually generate warm feelings? Will a bitter-free acceptance develop through loving actions extended toward an offending mate?

To recognize the limits of the "feelings flow from action" model, recall the flow chart in Figure 2. The sequence begins with a significant interpersonal Event, moves through the Primary Emotional Response to Evaluation of Event, and then goes to the Secondary Emotional Response. There are five major points sketched in that figure:

1. People respond to significant interpersonal events with both a *decision* and an *emotion.*

2. The decision may be to *minister* in spite of an offense or to *manipulate* because of an offense and the hurt it provoked; because the decision represents a free choice, we must bear full responsibility for the alternative we select.

3. The primary (or immediate) emotional response to a significant event will be either *enjoyment* or *displeasure.* Which of the two emotions we feel depends entirely on the nature of the event; because we have no control over which emotion we experience, we must accept no responsibility (credit or blame) for feeling either one.

4. The primary emotional response to an event shifts quickly into a secondary (or mediate) emotional response, a feeling that can be either sinful or nonsinful:

    a. Enjoyment can become *dependency* (sinful) or *satisfaction* (nonsinful);

    b. Displeasure can become *bitterness* (sinful) or *disappointment* (nonsinful).

5. Whether a primary emotion develops into a sinful or nonsinful secondary emotion depends *not* on the nature of the event, but on the *evaluation* of it:

    a. If we evaluate an *enjoyable event* as relevant to our *needs*, our secondary emotion will be *dependency*.

    b. If we evaluate an *enjoyable event* as relevant to our *desires*, our secondary emotion will be *satisfaction*.

    c. If we evaluate a *displeasurable event* as relevant to our *needs*, our secondary emotion will be *bitterness*.

    d. If we evaluate a *displeasurable event* as relevant to our *desires*, our *secondary emotion* will be *disappointment*.

Consider again what happens when a person is offended. The event requires a decision (which may feel like a reflex), and the event generates an emotion. Assume that Bill, the offended husband, truly wants to accept his offending wife Mary. Suppose he decides to forgive and tries to forget.

If his decision to forgive represents a sincere choice rather than a pressured concession to duty, Bill will inflict no intentional reprisals against his wife. But this choice is not easily made. Suppose Mary's offense was repeated infidelity. Because she genuinely repented, Bill decided to forgive her and work at rebuilding the marriage. During counseling, Bill related that he often "shared" with his wife how devastated he feels whenever he recalls her adultery.

"Isn't it right to share my feelings with Mary?" he asked.

"It depends upon your *purpose* in sharing your feelings," I answered. "Everything you do must fall within the framework of one purpose, and that is ministry. Telling Mary that you are struggling with memories of her sin heaps guilt and frustration on her. I suspect that you really intend your 'sharing' to be a punishing consequence for what she has done. But your decision to forgive and to minister requires that you not mention your hurt feelings again."

The first element in forgiveness is a firm decision to impose no penalty for the offense, and this includes an alert sensitivity to the subtle ways that decision can be contradicted.

After Bill understands and implements the decision aspect of forgiveness, he may still have the problem of handling his feelings and being able to forget.

"What do I do with all those angry, hurt feelings inside? I can force myself to make love to Mary, but I can't help thinking about her in bed with another man. It's more than I can handle! It makes me lose all interest in sex. Sometimes I lose my erection and can't perform at all. Even if I'm able to continue with intercourse, Mary is aware—very aware—that something is wrong. How can I put these thoughts out of my mind? Until I'm able to not think about her affair, or at least not get upset when I do think about it, I can't see how I'll ever be able to really accept Mary."

At this point I question whether a consistent attitude of forgiveness is enough to neutralize the memory of the offense. Consider what happens if Bill attempts to labor under the conviction that his memory will eventually fade.

If Bill feels bitter and upset, his difficulty involves a wrong evaluation of the event of his wife's infidelity. The primary emotion of displeasure has developed into bitterness, because Bill incorrectly believes that the offending event bears implications for his adequacy as a male. The cure for his bitterness, then, is not *rededicated effort* but *renewed thinking*. His bitterness will remain unless he learns to regard his wife's sin as a block to what he wants rather than as a threat to what he needs. No amount of "forgiving behaviors" can directly change the bitterness into disappointment because the immediate cause of the bitterness is a wrong evaluation of the event, not wrong behavioral responses to the event.

Suppose however that Bill persists in his decision to be forgiving without correcting his faulty evaluation. What will happen to the bitterness? Many would argue that the resentful feelings might eventually be repressed, and they would warn about the danger of these malignant emotions surfacing in other ways. But as I understand psychological functioning, it is technically more correct to state that *memories of events* are repressed, not *feelings about events*. The point, though technical, is important.

Emotions are not repressible. We may fail to discharge physical tensions experienced as emotions, and this may be called "emotional repression"; but emotions—the intangible, motivating states of subjective awareness—cannot themselves be repressed. Although emotions cannot be repressed, thoughts can be. The memory of the event that triggers the emotion can be denied attention. We can simply keep our mind off it. We can choose not to dwell on the troubling event, motivated by a desire not to experience the pain the memory stimulates. With practice, we can become quite proficient in selectively attending to more pleasant (or at least less painful) thoughts.[4]

But what does such repression accomplish? As long as Bill continues to regard Mary's adultery as damaging to his significance as a male, he has failed to grasp what it means to trust the Lord in this situation. His flesh-inspired conviction that Mary's respect is essential to his self-acceptance remains unchallenged; consequently the idolatrous purpose to meet needs through someone other than Christ will still control him.

The counselor who merely instructs his bitter client to decide to forgive the offending partner has failed to promote the maturity that comes through relying on Christ alone. He has succeeded only in fostering a dutiful approach to ministry which stagnates the couple far short of the goal of oneness in Christ. Beneath Bill's renewed efforts to treat Mary kindly will lie a hollow sense that something is just not right. Greater determination is an incomplete strategy for promoting the oneness that requires true acceptance. A renewed mind—changed evaluation of the disturbing event—is necessary.

If rigidly honoring a decision to forgive fails to address the problems of repressed memories (memories that retain the power to generate bitter feelings), what is the solution? The missing element is reevaluating the event to see it as God sees it—as unfortunate but irrelevant to one's security and significance. Making the shift from the wrong perspective to the right one is central to the work of forgiveness.

The Work of Forgiveness: What It Requires

True forgiveness differs from incomplete forgiveness in its evaluation of the offending event as relevant to one's desire for loving companionship rather than to one's needs for security and significance. The key to "forgetting" an offending event is a reevaluation of the event until it is seen as not especially important to one's purposes. Bitterness will give way to disappointment (which is acceptable) if the firm *decision* to forgive is accompanied by Spirit-led *meditation* on the truth that needs are fully met in Christ.

---

[4] It might be helpful to point out that when nagging memories of a maddening event have revenge as their theme, they are often defensive cover-ups for the memory of the disturbing event itself and the profound hurt it occasioned. It is less painful to be angry than hurt.

NO FORGIVENESS

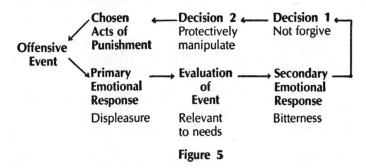

Figure 5

INCOMPLETE FORGIVENESS

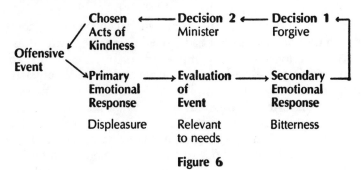

Figure 6

TRUE FORGIVENESS

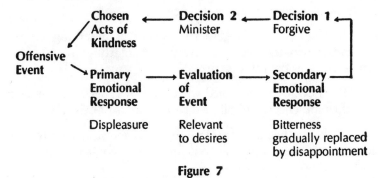

Figure 7

We need to examine the process of reevaluating offensive events to see them as hurtful, but not harmful. Let me repeat the statement that introduced this section:

> The experience of accepting your spouse depends on the work of forgiveness, which in turn depends on a willingness to see the offensive behavior of your spouse in biblical context.

Bill, still struggling with bitterness, shouts, "I'm willing! I'm willing to reevaluate Mary's offense so I can be fully forgiving. How do I do it?" Bill's question asks how we can learn to attribute a new meaning to an event.

The answer lies in a principle that may appear complicated but is really quite simple: *The meaning of an event is determined by its perceived context.* To put it another way, I will evaluate an event's significance in terms of the context in which the event occurs.

Suppose my wife says the words, "Will you please go away!" The meaning these words have for me will depend upon the context in which they are spoken. If I had arrived home unexpectedly as she was in the living room wrapping a gift for me, her words would mean one thing. If she asked me to leave after an especially heated disagreement, however, her words would have different meaning.

With this principle in mind, consider how placing a disturbing event in biblical context will alter the meaning of that event. People who regard an offending event as relevant to personal needs typically commit three errors in wrapping a context around the event:

1. They fail to realize (be deeply aware of) that Christ's love makes them secure and that being caught up in Christ's purposes provides them with true significance;

2. They tend to regard themselves as deserving of better treatment than they have received, apparently unaware of what justice requires of sinful man;

3. They are preoccupied with their own needs to the degree that they are effectively blinded to the needs of others.

To learn that an offending event is relevant merely to our desires, this event must be thought of in a context that corrects each of these errors:

1. We must grasp the truth that our needs are met in Christ by meditating on our riches in Him, aggressively telling ourselves that

we are worthwhile even when we feel most rejected and useless, and choosing to live in a manner that reflects our position. Searching the Scriptures and contemplating our findings is essential. When our minds visualize what our spouses did to us, we must forcefully remind ourselves that whatever has happened does not alter the fact that I am secure in Christ's love and significant in His plan. The key is never to allow the memory of an offending event to run through our minds without immediately restating to ourselves the truth of "needs met in Christ."

2. We must reflect on the degree to which we have been forgiven. In Matthew 18:21-35, our Lord commands us to forgive each other from the heart. The theme of the passage is that forgiveness of others should flow naturally from an awareness and appreciation of how much God has forgiven us. We must never demand better treatment on grounds of what we deserve; our lives merit eternal punishment. Yet God has forgiven us and granted us eternal joy. Reflection on the sins that God has forgiven must provide context for memories of our partners' offensive behavior. Only one who appreciates God's forgiveness can truly forgive others.

3. Paul instructs us to look out for the interests of others, regarding them as more important than ourselves (Phil. 2:3-4). Whenever Bill remembers Mary's infidelity, he must insist on thinking also about Mary's needs. Rather than focusing on how her behavior affects him (looking out for himself), he must choose to reflect on the struggles Mary may be experiencing (looking out for her).

This is difficult. People are adept at recognizing their own hurts and maintaining an academic distance from another's pain: "I'm sure she is hurting, but what about me? I'm hurting too!"

How quickly your mood changes when your mate, who offended you earlier in the day, is rushed to the hospital with severe chest pains. When we can see our partners not merely as people who sometimes hurt us, but as people with hurts of their own, our attitude will slowly shift from regarding their offense as monumental to recognizing it as trivial in light of our opportunity to minister to their needs.

Such an awareness will never develop without a firm decision to forgive and to minister. The work of forgiveness begins with a decision but continues with reevaluation.

Two final diagrams will summarize the discussion:

**Unbiblical Context Reinforces
Wrong Evaluation of Offending Event**

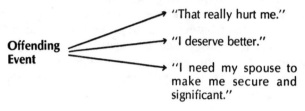

Figure 8

**Biblical Context Reinforces
Right Evaluation of Offending Event**

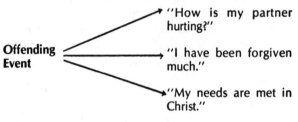

Figure 9

CONCLUSION

Building Block 3 is acceptance. To accept our mates does not require that we enjoy everything they do. To accept our mates means more than remaining faithful to the commitment to minister. To accept a mate involves deeper work than the decision to forgive when offended.

True acceptance requires a willingness to be vulnerable, to give oneself in a way that opens up avenues for painful rejection. To achieve this acceptance, we must continually forgive our partners when they hurt us. And the work of forgiveness requires that we regard the worst our partners can do as absolutely irrelevant to our basic personal needs. With that truth fixed in our minds, we will be able to minister freely to our spouses, without fear or pressure, even when they have offended us. This defines accepting one's spouse.

In defining Total Oneness as the blueprint of marriage and describing the three building blocks that stand on the foundation, we have left many questions unanswered. These questions deal with the responsibilities of each partner in reaching toward oneness:

What does it mean to submit to one's husband?

Does headship give husbands the right to make decisions for their wives?

What are some practical ways to promote better communica-tion, to help a wife feel loved and a husband important?

When a barrier goes up between a couple, how does it get torn down? Should they talk out the problem? Who goes first? Suppose one partner won't open up.

These and other questions will be dealt with in another book as we strive for Total Oneness in marriage.